THE WILD KNIGHT OF BATTERSEA

He who praises a man ought to follow him, and if he be not ready to follow him he ought not to praise him.
—*St. John Chrysostom*

MODERN CHRISTIAN REVOLUTIONARIES

THE WILD KNIGHT OF BATTERSEA:
G. K. CHESTERTON

By

F. A. LEA

When corruption and chaos are disturbing ordinary minds and many good men are only worried and serious, it has often happened that a great man could apparently be frivolous; and appear in history almost as a great buffoon.
—G. K. CHESTERTON: *Chaucer*

WIPF & STOCK · Eugene, Oregon

Wipf and Stock Publishers
199 W 8th Ave, Suite 3
Eugene, OR 97401

The Wild Knight of Battersea
G. K. Chesterton
By Lea, F. A.
Copyright©1945 James Clarke Lutterworth Press
ISBN 13: 978-1-5326-8440-1
Publication date 3/10/2019
Previously published by James Clarke & Co., LTD., 1945

BIBLIOGRAPHY

The following works of G. K. Chesterton have been chiefly drawn upon in this study:

The Defendant, (Dent, 1901).
Twelve Types, (Humphreys, 1902).
Browning, (Macmillan, 1903).
The Napoleon of Notting Hill, (Lane, 1904).
Heretics, (Lane, 1905).
Charles Dickens, (Methuen, 1906).
The Man who was Thursday, (Methuen, 1908).
Orthodoxy, (Lane, 1908).
Tremendous Trifles, (Methuen, 1909).
George Bernard Shaw, (Lane, 1910).
What's Wrong with the World, (Cassell, 1910).
The Victorian Age in Literature, (Butterworth, 1913).
The Flying Inn, (Methuen, 1914).
The New Jerusalem, (Hodder & Stoughton, 1920).
The Superstition of Divorce, (Chatto & Windus, 1920).
Eugenics and Other Evils, (Cassell, 1922).
The Man Who Knew Too Much, (Cassell, 1922).
The Outline of Sanity, (Methuen, 1926).
St. Francis of Assisi, (Hodder & Stoughton, 1926).
The Thing, (Sheed & Ward, 1929).
The Poet and the Lunatics, (Cassell, 1929).
Come to Think of It, (Methuen, 1931).
Chaucer, (Faber & Faber, 1932).
St. Thomas Aquinas, (Hodder & Stoughton, 1933).
All I Survey, (Methuen, 1935).
Autobiography, (Hutchinson, 1936).
Collected Poems, (Methuen, 1937).
The End of the Armistice, (Sheed & Ward, 1939).

1

It was G. K. Chesterton's life-long fate to be taken seriously when he was being flippant, and flippantly when he was being serious. Since he very seldom was flippant, he was nearly always laughed at, alike by his friends and enemies. They admired or admitted him as a "character", and there, too often, criticism has been allowed to stay. The memory of him cherished by the world is summed up in Mr. Walter de la Mare's portrait of Falstaff:

"He smiled, compact of loam, this orchard man."

Reformers shook their heads over him: he seemed constitutionally unable to treat reform as the serious matter it was; conservatives applauded his "magnificent common sense": they who would never have dreamed of trying to revive the village-community, let alone wearing sombrero hats. The solemn were offended by his frivolity; the frivolous were shocked by his solemnity: neither knew what to make of him. Both seized on the aspect of his writing that appealed to them, called that the "essential Chesterton", dismissed the rest as playful perversity; neither could escape an uncomfortable suspicion that the essential Chesterton was all the time chuckling at them from behind another tree, while they clasped his empty coat in their hands. He fell between dozens of stools. His friends, seeing him fall, rushed to the rescue, to plant him firmly on the stool nearest themselves. But he did not seem to appreciate their help; he only fell over again on the other side, like the White Knight; and in the end they also gave him up as a bad job. They left him to the multitude; and the multitude, which has no ideas, was content to look up to him as a huge, benign figure; a sort of universal uncle officiating at a never-ending Christmas party; an old gentleman so obviously charming that, said they, he must really be like themselves, whatever quaint views it might amuse him to profess.

However, to be a character is by no means the same thing as to have one. Indeed, university dons make a point of metamorphosing themselves into "characters" expressly in order to conceal the fact that they have none. It is the only way they can draw attention to themselves. They inhabit universities for the same reason: they are the only places where they would be noticed. Even to have "no character" in the poet's sense may be a potent incentive towards becoming one. For to lack identity is to be the plaything of other people's opinions; it is to be acutely sensitive to other people's regard: and one so sensitive cannot but hold his popularity a matter of life and death. A "character" is a passport to popularity, a nickname the first step on the way to a name.

That Chesterton was a character is a truism. That he was enormously popular is equally true. And the essays which, more than anything else, established his fame are reminiscent of Mr. Dick's soap-bubbles, alike in their iridescence and their reflection of a child-like personality. It is impossible to dislike Mr. Dick, even when one of his soap-bubbles gets in your eye. It was equally impossible (for most people) to take offence at G. K. Chesterton, exulting in the *Daily News* over dragons, Easter-eggs and Christmas. Like Browning, "He delighted, with a true poetic delight, in being conventional. Being by birth an Englishman, he took pleasure in being an Englishman; being by rank a member of the middle class, he took a pride in its ancient scruples and its everlasting boundaries. He was everything he was with a definite and conscious pleasure" (*Browning*). He enjoyed his popularity, and enjoyed himself—literally, as one might enjoy a glass of ale or a circus: nobody can laugh at Chesterton without laughing with him. And it was by this "ardent and headstrong conventionality" that he fulfilled that ambition to "belong" which must have been with him even as a boy, when he strove manfully to remain at the bottom of his form at St. Paul's.

Nevertheless, the laughter and applause that warmed his heart never went to his head. He began his career, like Gabriel Syme in *The Man who was Thursday*, by "revolting into sanity", for the sake of revolt, and because there was nothing else left to revolt into. But this youthful pose was quickly superseded by a real and deep-seated revolution and reorientation of his whole standpoint. His "character" was at no time afterwards the most important thing about him in his own eyes, whatever it may have been in others'. Before he had a public, he had ceased to depend on public opinion. Underlying all his apparent perversities was the consistency of a real conviction, without which they would have been as empty, as well as brilliant, as soap-bubbles. "I know nothing", he wrote, "so contemptible as a mere paradox; a mere ingenious defence of the indefensible . . . Mr. Shaw is cruelly hampered by the fact that he cannot tell any lie unless he thinks it is the truth. I find myself under the same intolerable bondage" (*Orthodoxy*). Mere consistency is essential to a "character"; conviction of truth is not. Consistency in perversity would have been enough to ensure Chesterton's popularity. He was not perverse. If he attacked what he believed to be the pedantry of Prussian professors, when public opinion held them in esteem, that did not prevent him from continuing to do so after the whole populace had rallied to his flag. His books, he said at the end of his life, he had never taken seriously: his opinions he had. Since one of the first of these was that an artist's success must be judged by his own standards, and not by what his critics think ought to have been his standards, Chesterton's must be measured at least as much by his wisdom as his wit.

§

He was one of the last important English men of letters to embrace orthodox Christianity *in toto* at an early age, and grow up inside it. That is the first essential fact about him. The book *Orthodoxy* was his confession of faith. It appeared as early as 1909, when he was thirty-five, and it contains nothing that he would have repudiated at any time afterwards. It was not, however, till long afterwards that it began to be taken seriously, and even then not by everybody. As late as 1929 he found it necessary to refute a critic in some modernist newspaper, who had said that "for all he knew" Mr. Chesterton was "modernist enough in his own thoughts". He shared the general fate of poets and prophets, and all who are pre-eminently gifted with the power to say what they mean: nobody would believe that he meant what he said. He told rationalists that they were irrational, but they only laughed; he told them that there was nothing to laugh at, and they laughed all the louder; then he grew angry, and they were hurt; they felt that he was letting them down. To dismiss Chesterton's conversion as a joke which may be carried too far, however, or as an elaborate parody on more solemn ecclesiasticism, is to make nonsense of his whole achievement; and though there are some who are quite prepared to do this, and even to justify their action on the ground that nonsense is what one looks for from a humorist, it must be insisted firmly that this conception of humour is too narrow:

that there is a kind of humour that is not nonsensical—and also a kind of nonsense that is not humorous. One can always forgive a man for not immediately locating the Great Nebula when a rocket is fired to show him where it is, or for losing sight of the argument of *Orthodoxy* in the illustrations; but no one who has himself experienced that sudden co-ordination of intuitions which we call conversion can really mistake the authenticity of the descriptions of it contained in that book, or fail finally to sympathize with the author when he throws in his hand in gay despair over the impossibility of expounding it: "There is, therefore, about all complete conviction, a kind of huge helplessness. The belief is so big that it takes a long time to get into action. And this hesitation chiefly arises, oddly enough, from an indifference about where one should begin."

§

In *Orthodoxy* "the main problem for philosophers" is defined as "how we can contrive at once to be astonished at the world and yet at home in it". Not many philosophers, I think, would acknowledge that as their main problem, or even as a problem at all. At any rate, they would say, it is necessary first to decide whether the world exists or astonishment is a possibility, and, if it is, whether it needs anybody to be astonished or anything to be astonished at. Chesterton poured ridicule on such enquiries. "Most modern philosophies", he said, "are not philosophy but philosophic doubt; that is, doubt about whether there can be any philosophy" (*St. Thomas Aquinas*). He accepted the old idea of philosophy as the pursuit of wisdom; and it is only within the circuit of that idea that his problem has any meaning. The question whether it is, in fact, "the main problem for philosophers" remains to be discussed. But one thing is certain: it had been the main problem for Chesterton himself.

He himself had never ceased to be astonished at the world. He had, he said in his *Autobiography*, preserved into manhood something of "the romance of receptivity" of a child. He had not come to take the world for granted. But he had, in growing up, been confronted by a system of reasoning, apparently impregnable, which denied the validity, and even the actuality, of his wonder. How, it challenged, could he be thankful for creation when there was nobody to thank, or be astonished at what was only a projection of his own imagination? It is hard to picture Chesterton at any time deeply impressed by the arguments of "nihilists"; yet he has left a record in two of his romances, *The Man who was Thursday* ("thrown up in the nihilism of the nineties") and *The Poet and the Lunatics*, of that "mood of unreality and sterile isolation" which, as he says in the autobiography, settled upon him under their influence. Says Gabriel Gale in *The Poet and the Lunatics*:

"I also dreamed that I had dreamed of the whole creation. I had given myself the stars for a gift; I had handed myself the sun and moon. I had been behind and at the beginning of all things; and without me nothing was made that was made. Anybody who has been in that centre of the cosmos knows that it is to be in hell."

Chesterton's had been a peculiar, but authentic, case of that division between the deductions of reason and the certainties of intuition which is the precondition of genuine conversion.

He had not ceased to be astonished at the world; but he had ceased to be at home in it. And this alienation, this sterile isolation afflicting him, was ended by one thing—Christianity. It was Christianity, or Christian theology, that supplied him with a system of reasoning as compact and comprehensive as anything the nihilists could offer, which yet had a place in it for all the experiences he valued: a place of honour indeed. It was Christianity that reconciled his reason with his intuition; and a Christian philosopher whose works he read, so he declared, with a pleasure "definitely not only of the reason, but also of the imagination".

The chapter in *Orthodoxy* entitled "The Maniac" is the most appropriate commentary on *The Poet and the Lunatics*. *Orthodoxy* itself is the record of Chesterton's conversion. And the *St. Thomas Aquinas* contains an account of the kind of life that sprang from it. If we accept his conception of philosophy as the pursuit of wisdom, there is but one way of answering the question whether "How we can contrive at once to be astonished at the world and yet at home in it" is really what he called it, "the main problem for philosophers": and that is by deciding whether this kind of life made him wise.

§

It was the life of the "great contemplative". The great contemplative, he said, "is the complete contrary of that false contemplative, the mystic who looks only into his own soul, the selfish artist who shrinks from the world and lives only in his own mind". He is one who faces outwards, and surrenders himself to each fresh object in turn of the outer world.

> "According to Aquinas the object becomes a part of the mind; nay, according to Aquinas the mind actually becomes the object. But, as one commentator

acutely puts it, it only becomes the object and does not create the object. In other words, the object *is* an object; it can and does exist outside the mind, or in the absence of the mind. And *therefore* it enlarges the mind of which it becomes a part. The mind conquers a new province like an emperor; but only because the mind has answered the bell like a servant."

One is reminded of the poet, who "is the most unpoetical of anything in existence, because he has no identity—he is continually in for and filling some other body" (Keats: Letter of Oct. 27, 1818). And it is just this attitude of more than intellectual humility, which he equated with the spontaneous "wonder" of children—the vision uncorrupted by theory or convention—that Chesterton made it his life-work to preach and practice. He continues:

"Note how this view avoids both pitfalls; the alternative abysses of impotence. The mind is not merely receptive, in the sense that it absorbs sensations like so much blotting-paper; on that sort of softness has been based all that cowardly materialism which conceives man as wholly servile to his environment. On the other hand, the mind is not purely creative, in the sense that it paints pictures on the windows and then mistakes them for the landscape outside. But the mind is active, and its activity consists in following, so far as the will chooses to follow, the light outside that does really shine upon real landscapes. . . . In other words, the essence of the thomist common sense is that two agencies are at work; reality and the recognition of reality; and their meeting is a sort of marriage. Indeed it is very truly a marriage, because it is fruitful; the only philosophy now in the world that really is fruitful."

THE WILD KNIGHT OF BATTERSEA 15

We can see how it was that the thomist philosophy came to Chesterton as a liberation, that it made "a very peculiar and powerful impression" upon him "analogous to poetry". It enabled him to adopt consciously towards the world an attitude that had previously been unconscious, or rather, instinctive and at variance with his intellect. Thereafter he could, and did, spend his life answering the bell like a servant and conquering innumerable provinces like an emperor. We can justly apply to himself his own further words concerning St. Thomas: "He was a man who always turned his full attention to anything; and he seems to fix even passing things as they pass. To him even what was momentary was momentous. The reader feels that any small point of economic habit or human accident is for the moment almost scorched under the converging rays of a magnifying lens". And furthermore: "It is impossible to put in these pages a thousandth part of the decisions on details of life that may be found in his work. . . . We can only touch on one or two obvious topics of this kind." This is to be an introduction to Chesterton and not a dissertation.

§

But, it will be said, there is nothing peculiarly orthodox about the attitude he has been describing. And that is true. There is a palpable equivocation contained in the passage we have just quoted. It is not the philosophy that is fruitful but the way of life promoted by it; and it is quite possible, nay, it is certain, that other philosophies besides the thomist (or Chestertonian) may solve the same problem and promote the same attitude. But Chesterton's intuitions, prior to his acceptance of orthodoxy, had been manifold: this had been only one of them. There had been others, demanding a far more elaborate rationalization. "This, therefore, is . . . my reason for accepting the religion and not merely the scattered and secular truths out of the religion. I do it because the thing has not merely told this truth or that truth, but has revealed itself as a truth-telling thing" (*Orthodoxy*). It substantiated and coordinated *all* his intuitions—and for a very obvious reason: because they were precisely the intuitions to substantiate and coordinate which it had originally been designed. It fitted him, because it had been measured to fit—like Cinderella's shoe; he did not have to chop off his toes or pad it with paper before he could get into it. He could wear it naturally—far more naturally than most theologians. He could, and did, caper in it, whilst they hobbled and limped; and when he wanted to use it as a weapon, he kicked with it: he did not have to take it off first and throw it. It had been the key to his difficulties, and when he saw others in the same difficulties he used it as a key: he did not knock them down with it, like St. Peter in the *Vision of Judgement*.

Naturally, he was misunderstood. People had grown so used to hearing church dogmas propounded dogmatically they had ceased to believe that they could really mean anything to anybody; they had grown so used to seeing them accepted as superstitions, they had forgotten that even superstitions often have a foundation in fact. "We and our critics have come to talk in two different languages; so that the very names by which we describe the things inside stand for totally different things in the absurd labels they have stuck upon the wall outside. Often if we said the great things we have to say, they would sound like the small things they accuse us of saying" (*The Thing*). He had to explain patiently to Mr. H. G. Wells that the dogma of The Fall rested on realities of experience, and could not be confuted simply by saying, "Where is the Garden of Eden?"

"There ought," he observed once, "to be a real study called anthropology corresponding to theology" (*St. Thomas Aquinas*). Orthodoxy interpreted his own nature to himself and thereby detached him from it. It was for this reason that he was able to call Aquinas an anthropologist: he had "a complete theory of Man, right or wrong". In his *St. Thomas Aquinas* Chesterton deplores the too exclusive attention given by modern anthropologists to the study of anthropoids. The science of man as it exists, he complains, leaves out of its scope precisely those features of man that are distinctive: those that distinguish *homo sapiens* from *simius insipiens*. Yet, "it is necessary to know whether he is responsible or irresponsible, perfect or imperfect, perfectible or unperfectible, mortal or immortal, doomed or free: not in order to understand God, but in order to understand Man. Nothing that leaves these things under a cloud of religious doubt can possibly pretend to be a Science of Man". In orthodoxy, and orthodoxy alone, he found these questions answered. They were answered so completely, and so completely to his satisfaction, that he concluded right away that the pronouncements of the Church on other issues, which had not yet faced him, were probably satisfactory also. At the end of *Orthodoxy* he declares that he is willing to accept them tentatively, until he has proved them by experience. By the time he had written *St. Thomas Aquinas* he had accepted them absolutely, without the proviso.

§

He became a Roman Catholic in 1922. Thereby he bound himself to accept as just and true whatever the supreme authority of the Roman Catholic Church pronounced—within however circumscribed a sphere—to be just and true. And thereby, I think, he made his first great error. He set himself apart from the religious tradition of his own country, and glanced aside the impact of his influence on its religious and political thought. Nor would he have repudiated these charges; he would only have added that they were not charges at all, but a commendation and a comparison. Nevertheless, his action betokened a certain insensitiveness to the ethical advances and contributions that really have been made by the Protestant churches in England: contributions, which have no parallel within the Roman Church, and which are, in fact, incompatible with its pretensions.

He was one of the most brilliant controversialists who have ever lived. In the *St. Thomas* he states the principle upon which his controversies were conducted: "We must either not argue with a man at all, or we must argue on his grounds and not ours." He was, in fact, continually engaged in cutting their ground from under his opponents' feet. While they aimed their big guns at some distant, and generally illusory, target, he would rise up suddenly behind them and turn their artillery upon themselves. Did they challengingly assert that "Living religion is not in dull and dusty dogmas"?—Of course it is not, he replied: but our dogmas are neither dull nor dusty. Did they arraign him as a reactionary, because he argued against their socialism?—"I do not object to socialism because it will revolutionize our commerce", he would answer blandly: "but because it will leave it so horribly the same." He always knew the standpoint of his opponents better than they knew it themselves—and far better than they knew his. Therein lies the advantage of being a controversialist of imagination: he had entered into their minds, and sympathized. None the less, on the one issue of ecclesiastical authority he was unable to employ his accustomed tactics. When he was told that he had surrendered his freedom of conscience, by subscribing in advance to the dictates of the infallible pope, he evaded the charge, first by proclaiming that there was as much, if not more, variety of opinion among Catholics than other men—*upon topics to which the dogma of infallibility did not extend;* and secondly, by asserting that he did no more in taking the verdicts of the Church on trust than other men did in accepting the facts laid out in a Bradshaw—an analogy too obviously false to need refutation.

Chesterton's allegiance to Rome was, we believe, his first great error. Nevertheless it was, in a sense, inevitable. He had one of the most naturally Catholic minds that have appeared in England during this century. That is to say, not only was he naturally religious, in the highest sense, and therefore bound to be attracted by the magnificent breadth and almost unlimited provisions of the Roman Catholic Church; but he was inclined from the first to submit his conscience to authority. We can detect this in his attitude to orthodox theology itself; it is epitomized in that little phrase, parenthetical in the passage we have quoted from his *St. Thomas*, "so far as the will chooses to follow".

We have said that he knew his opponents' viewpoints better than they knew them themselves. This is strictly true, so long as his opponents were rationalists, modernists, progressive humanitarians and so forth. He reasserted and substantiated repeatedly his claim that "the modern world, with its modern movements, is living on its Catholic capital"; that is to say, that one "progressive" movement after another since the Reformation has seized upon some single element out of the old Catholic synthesis, and built upon it as upon a self-evident truth; whereas, not only was it already contained in Catholicism, together with many other elements equally important (without which it was itself no more than a half—or even quarter—truth), but that apart from the total philosophy it was not self-evident at all. For example:

> "The Calvinists took the Catholic idea of the absolute knowledge and power of God; and treated it as a rocky irreducible truism so solid that anything could be built on it, however crushing or cruel. They were so confident in their logic, and its one first principle of predestination, that they tortured the intellect and imagination with dreadful deductions about God, that seemed to turn Him into a demon. But it never seems to have struck them that somebody might suddenly say that he did not believe in the demon" (*The Thing*).

Similarly Shelley and Whitman and the revolutionary optimists of the eighteenth century:

> "They also, though less consciously because of the chaos of their times, had really taken out of the old Catholic tradition one particular transcendental idea; the idea that there is a spiritual dignity in man as man, and a universal duty to love men as men. And they acted in exactly the same extraordinary way as their prototypes, the Wesleyans and the Calvinists. They took it for granted that this spiritual idea was absolutely self-evident like the sun and moon; that nobody could ever destroy that, though in the name of it they destroyed everything else. They perpetually hammered away at their human divinity and human dignity, and inevitable love for all human beings; as if these things

were naked natural facts. And now they are quite surprised when new and restless realists suddenly explode, and begin to say that a pork-butcher with red whiskers and a wart on his nose does not strike them as particularly divine or dignified, that they are not conscious of the smallest sincere impulse to love him, that they could not love him if they tried, or that they do not recognize any particular obligation to try" (*op. cit*).

The modern world "is using, and using up, the truths that remain to it out of the old treasury of Christendom". The point itself is urgent. For, as Chesterton did not fail to point out, this process may well be carried to its logical conclusion, in the repudiation of pity itself, the last of the traditional virtues. It is a conclusion that does not seem so remote from us to-day as it may have done in 1929 A.D. And there is nothing, nothing whatever, to prevent it, except the promulgation of a true philosophy in which all these truths and virtues find their place and their justification. If they are to be challenged by reason, they must be reasonably defended: the unaided instinct can no longer be trusted to uphold them. Yet, just when they are most needed, because they are most needed, there is a real and desperate danger of the world's losing sight of *all* the forms and systems in which they have hitherto inhered, and all the symbols the past has established to convey them to the imaginations of men. Of this danger Chesterton was acutely aware. It was because he was aware of it that he pitted himself hand and foot against all the partial and logically indefensible positions taken up by his Protestant and humanitarian critics. It was *not* sufficient, he saw clearly, to take this virtue or that virtue out of the treasury of Christendom and call it the one thing necessary: it was not sufficient either to earn the title of "Christian" or to save Christianity itself. It was a case of all or nothing. And we can see how truly great must have been the temptation to him of an authoritarian church which, as he believed, stood for the all, and used its authority to enforce it. The Roman Catholic Church may possibly thrust itself in the way of new and acceptable ideas; but it does certainly stand out against the endless proliferation of old and unacceptable ones. The papacy has never tolerated, as the Protestant churches have had to tolerate, the anti-intellectual pragmatism of Buchman.

Still, Chesterton's assumption that the Catholic theology was "all" remained an assumption—and one which he refused to question. That is the crux of the argument. He had no difficulty in dealing with the representatives of movements based on scattered and secular truths out of his own religion: because he accepted their basic principles himself, and a great deal more besides. But he could not, or would not, admit that there was any positive significance in the original repudiation of the Catholic synthesis from which they sprang. Yet it was not mere perversity that brought about the Reformation; it was not even sheer indignation alone, against the monstrous iniquities of the papal curia at the time of the Renaissance. It would be truer to say that it was the Renaissance itself. Chesterton could point out the need of a complete anthropology, corresponding to theology, and demonstrate that all his opponents' were incomplete; but he would not allow that such a complete anthropology might really be found outside Catholicism. From the first he followed only so far as his will chose to follow the light outside that did really shine upon real things; and his will did not choose to follow the light that shone upon certain things. He acknowledged the existence of a complete anthropology that rested on faith in the supernatural, and of many incomplete anthropologies that repudiated the supernatural; he never seriously admitted the possibility of an anthropology that repudiated the supernatural and was yet complete. When he was faced with what some would regard as the potentiality of such a thing, he averted his eyes.[1]

It is significant that he at no time faced up fairly to the pantheist position. He was continually referring both to pantheism and Buddhism. In the *St. Thomas Aquinas* he repeatedly contrasts them with thomism: and always he dismisses them upon the same ground—that they deny the multiplicity whilst exalting the unity of creation. Had he ever submitted himself to the writings of either the pantheists of the western world or the Buddhists of the eastern, he might have discovered some things that would have made him pause. He might, for example, have discovered the following passage from an old *zen*, which, were the word "Catholicism" only substituted for "Buddhism", might easily be mistaken for one of his own familiar pronouncements:

"To a man who knows nothing of Buddhism, mountains are mountains, waters are waters, and trees are trees. But when he has read the scriptures and knows a little of Buddhism, mountains are no longer mountains, waters are no longer waters, and trees no longer trees (*i.e.*, they are *maya*, or illusion). But when he has thoroughly understood Buddhism, mountains are once again mountains, waters are waters, and trees are trees" (Quoted in *The Legacy of Asia and Western Man*, by A. W. Watts, Murray, 1937).

One is tempted to draw a further comparison between Chesterton's "wonder" and the "awe before the pure

[1] See Note I at the end of this book.

phenomenon" of the spinozist, Goethe; and between the attitude of "the great contemplative" and that "true process of subjective growth through objective experience", which has been ascribed to Goethe by Mr. Middleton Murry. But there is no object in emphasizing further what we believe to have been the limitations of Chesterton's Christianity. Whether we call it "awe" or "wonder", the recognition of whose importance he called the "chief idea" of his life, he himself certainly possessed it; and it is upon his manifestation of it, and the unique quality of that manifestation, that his claim to greatness reposes.

§

Chesterton, in *The Victorian Age in Literature*, once provoked a storm of indignation by likening Thomas Hardy to "the village atheist brooding and blaspheming over the village idiot" (a writer in *The Adelphi* called it a "most profoundly irreligious criticism"). To his accusers, however, he replied characteristically that this was not an attack on Hardy but a defence of him: for "the whole case for him is that he had the sincerity and simplicity of the village atheist". We might, I think, without being one whit more insulting, compare Chesterton in passing this judgement to the village idiot brooding and blaspheming over the village atheist. For it was precisely his truth and his triumph that he himself possessed something of the naïvety of the village idiot. Indeed, one might go so far as to draw a parallel between the English expression "a natural" and Goethe's *eine Natur*.

Another characteristic of the "natural" is often his irrepressible hilarity in grave situations. It is a characteristic that has been known to cause considerable resentment in the more solemn quarters of the community. Chesterton's much-needed emphasis on the place held by "wonder" in Christianity was his first important contribution to contemporary thought. His second, and more original, was the equation of wonder with humour.

It would nearly be true to say that this was his unique contribution. It is certainly true that no Christian philosopher has given it a more prominent place in his system. Goethe would probably have repudiated it altogether. Yet it is a great and necessary element in Christianity. Humour is, indeed, allied to forgiveness, because it is, as Clutton Brock once said, a "joyful sense of the imperfections of this life". Jesus's own love is hardly more perfectly manifested than in his nickname for James and John, "the Sons of Thunder". When he laughed at their ambition to call down fire from heaven upon the Samaritan village, he forgave in them what was nothing less than their complete incomprehension of everything that he stood for. He was laughing at his own despair.

It is by this quality of joyfulness that humour is distinguished from satire. Satire is essentially joyless. It is a bitter, merciless *denunciation* of what is imperfect; and it is the work of a man who is at heart miserable, because he is alone: as Swift and Byron and Heine were alone and miserable. It is the work of a man who has identified himself with the Good, aspired to the loneliness of God—and found the everlasting solitude of Satan. Satire is not life-bringing, however often it may deceive itself into thinking it is. It is deathly, because it calls into being the resentment it is bred of, and perpetuates it.

All this stripping away of illusions which is the principle occupation of "intellectuals" to-day is, in fine, but an indulgence of the supreme illusion: that of their own superiority. "The poetry", said Wilfred Owen, "is in the pity." Cynicisms of this sort cannot even be called pity turned rancid, for those who exhibit it have never attained to pity—or charity: they are the same thing. "They have not gone off their heads", one can hear Chesterton saying: "they have gone off their hearts; they have gone onto their heads: probably they were dropped on them in infancy—and they have been swollen ever since." To meet what is hateful with hate is to meet it on its own level, and duplicate it. Only by loving it, in all its hatefulness, can we hope to triumph over it, in spirit or in fact: for it is true, as Chesterton maintained—and he never uttered a truer paradox—that "until we love a thing in all its ugliness we cannot make it beautiful" (*Twelve Types*).

Thus he was unjust in calling Dickens "a violent satirist":

> "Nearly half-way through the nineteenth century there came out of England the voice of a violent satirist. In its political quality it seemed like the half-choked cry of the frustrated republic. It had no patience with the pretence that England was already free, that we had gained all that was valuable from the revolution. It poured a cataract of contempt on the so-called working compromises of England, on the oligarchic cabinets, on the two artificial parties, on the government offices, on the J.P.'s, on the vestries, on the voluntary charities. This satirist was Dickens, and it must be remembered that he was not only fierce, but uproariously readable. He really damaged the things he struck at, a very rare thing" (*Dickens*).

THE WILD KNIGHT OF BATTERSEA

Chesterton here is plainly thinking at least as much of himself as of Dickens. These were the abuses he also struck at. His "fiercest mood" also was "reserved for methods that were counted scientific and progressive".[1] It is possible that he also really damaged them. He was certainly uproariously readable. But it is just this quality of uproariousness in his work that distinguishes it from satire, in the sense in which we have been using the term. He laughed at the evils he decried even while he was tilting at them. Swift could never do that.

§

So Chesterton wrote *The Napoleon of Notting Hill*. It is the epic of the reconquest of London by humour and love, personified in Auberon Quin and Adam Wayne respectively. And the first important thing to notice about them is their child-like character—it is a feature that is repeatedly stressed; the second is the quality of vision with which both are invested. This is how Quin is introduced:

> "So the short government official looked at the coat-tails of the tall government official, and through street after street, and round corner after corner, saw only coat-tails, coat-tails, and again coat-tails—when, he did not in the least know why, something happened to his eyes.
> "Two black dragons were walking backwards in front of him. Two black dragons were looking at him with evil eyes. The dragons were walking backwards it was true, but they kept their eyes fixed on

[1] Especially *Eugenics and other Evils* and *The Fallacy of Divorce*.

him none the less. The eyes which he saw were, in truth, only the two buttons at the back of a frock-coat: perhaps some traditional memory of their meaningless character gave this half-witted prominence to their gaze. The slit between the tails was the nose-line of the monster: whenever the tails flapped in the winter wind the dragons licked their lips. It was only a momentary fancy, but the small clerk found it embedded in his soul ever afterwards. He never could again think of men in frock-coats except as dragons walking backwards."

The passage deserves to be quoted at length, because it illustrates a reservation we must make before going farther. "It was only a momentary fancy," says Chesterton. It would have been truer to say that the impression was only a fancy. For this seeing of things as *other than they are* is not quite what is meant by imaginative vision; it is not what he himself had meant by it. The alliance of Adam Wayne and Auberon Quin is capable of two alternative interpretations. Chesterton seldom distinguished them. Under the grave, yet humorous, seeing of a child he grouped a whole assemblage of attitudes, most of which may be valuable, but only one of which is indispensable.

In his second collection of essays, for example, there is a third: "Now I deny most energetically that anything is, or can be, uninteresting. So I stared at the joints in the walls and seats, and began thinking hard on the fascinating subject of wood. Just as I had begun to realize why, perhaps, it was that Christ was a carpenter . . ." (*Tremendous Trifles*). Blake is reported to have said that he could stare at a knot in a piece of wood until it terrified him; and Chesterton is fond of applying the adjective "terrible" to things: to pillar-boxes, railway-signals, human nature, etc. (In fact he did so far too often: the mannerism soon ceases to surprise and only irritates the reader). But in this case he is not *contemplating* a piece of wood at all—as Blake was, imaginatively; he is *thinking about* it; and not even thinking about a particular joint or knot, but about wood in general. The distinction is important; but it was not until the end of his life that he made it unequivocally. In his *Autobiography* occur the finest of his descriptions of childish vision. In this book occur also the following words:

> "I am much more disposed *now* to fancy that an apple-tree in the moonlight is some sort of ghost or grey nymph; or to see the furniture fantastically changing and crawling at twilight, as in some story of Poe or Hawthorne. But when I was a child I had a sort of confident astonishment in contemplating the apple-tree as an apple-tree."

The distinction was made too late. The "chief ideas" of Chesterton's life had, in fact, been two: first to reveal the necessity of direct perception; and secondly to disguise the revelation as completely as possible by confounding it with something totally different. No one would wish to conjure his fancy, any more than his character, out of existence. But, if the truth he proclaimed is to be given its due importance, they must be distinguished.

One purpose of these pages might be defined as that of rescuing Chesterton from "G.K." For I believe that Chesterton unconsciously distorted the doctrine of "becoming as a little child" to suit the exuberances of his character. It was "G.K.", the "orchard man", who rode through Beaconsfield breaking eggs down his shirt-front in the likeness of Dr. Johnson; who declared, and demonstrated, that direct was crooked seeing, that becoming child-like meant being childish; and who would, if he could, have equated the Kingdom of God with the Nurseries of Heaven.

2

THERE was a time when one of the regular Saturday afternoon entertainments arranged for Englishmen was a debate between G. K. Chesterton and Bernard Shaw. It is not recorded that agreement was ever reached on these occasions. Wine and water mingle badly; and it is, in fact, still a subject of dispute which rose to the top. Whatever the ultimate verdict, however, Chesterton's critical study of Shaw will remain a masterpiece. Nobody who has not read the whole of this book can fully appreciate the humour of the "defence" with which it ends: "To represent Shaw as profane or provocatively indecent is not a matter for discussion at all; it is a disgusting criminal libel upon a particularly respectable gentleman of the middle classes, of refined tastes and somewhat puritanical views."

Unless the truth in that description is recognized—and the rest of the study is written to substantiate it—the humour is lost. This points to the error of those who call Chesterton "perverse". Perversity by itself is not humorous at all. It only becomes so when it is consistent, with itself and with the truth. Neither Chesterton nor Shaw would have been wits had they not first been crusaders—any more than Johnson or Voltaire: or, if they had been, their aphorisms would long ago have been lost sight of, as have all but a few of Oscar Wilde's. Their settled convictions alone gave them the high and and secure vantage-ground from which to shoot: and held between their two fires, it would have been a hard road that journalists trod—had either of them ever been taken seriously.

Describing the impact of Bernard Shaw upon the literary world left over from the 'nineties, Chesterton compressed books into one phrase: "The single eye-glass fled before the single eye." Were we to describe his own collision with a world that centred upon Shaw, it could hardly be done better than by saying that the single eye itself recoiled. For that was the eye of an intellectual; and Chesterton came equipped with the two eyes of a child. The decadent with the single eye-glass had been doubly removed from reality; but the progressive with the single eye was still removed. He could see things from one side only—from the left. The child sees them from the left and right simultaneously.

Chesterton possessed the direct, imaginative vision of a child, and it is this that makes his greatness, as it does that of nearly all really great men: for the power to see things, not as we have been brought up to see them, nor as our preconceived theories demand that we should see them, but as they actually are, is the privilege of creative genius. Many have seen that this is true in the realm of art; and it was in that realm that Chesterton himself most often emphasized the truth.

> "The arts exist, as we should put it in our primeval fashion, to show forth the glory of God; or, to translate the same thing in terms of our psychology, to awaken and keep alive the sense of wonder in man. The success of any work of art is achieved when we say of any subject, a tree or a cloud or a human character, ' I have seen that a thousand times and I never saw it before '" (*The Thing*).

Nevertheless, the power to see things as they are is not confined to artists. Those who have the "vision and the faculty divine" are far outnumbered by those who have the vision only. And strange as it may seem, it is to the latter that I would most naturally assimilate Chesterton.

§

That Chesterton possessed genius is unquestionable; that he possessed an incomparable and astonishing eloquence nobody who has read or heard him would be prepared to deny; that he possessed that gift which, in poetry, Robert Bridges called the "highest of all"—"the power of concentrating all the far-reaching resources of language on one point, so that a single and apparently effortless expression rejoices the aesthetic imagination at the moment when it is most expectant and most exacting and at the same time astonishes the intellect with a new aspect of the truth" (*Collected Essays*, iv. "Critical Introduction to Keats")—that, I do not think anyone would claim for him. Chesterton astonishes the intellect often enough—too often, indeed, as I shall try to show: the final felicity is wanting.

He himself might have found it hard to admit this fact. He very often undertook to describe simple objects —a bird, a house, a chair—and very often he succeeded in describing them in such a way as to arouse our dormant imaginations: a bird he would define as "a blossom broken loose from its chain of stalk"; a house as "a gigantesque hat to cover a man from the sun"; a chair as "an apparatus of four wooden legs for a cripple with only two". In all these fantastic comparisons we can trace his effort to communicate his own renewed delight in everyday things. But it is precisely because we can trace his effort that Chesterton fails in his purpose. It is the author who startles us by his ingenuity, not the object by its novelty.

As with simple objects, so with the scenes in his romances. Let us take an example:

> "The man still holding the sword cast it down with a wordless sound more shocking than a curse. He was a tall, elegant man, with an air of fashion even in his duelling undress; his face, with a rather fine aquiline profile, looked whiter against red hair and a red pointed beard. The man beside him put a hand upon his shoulder and seemed to push him a little, perhaps urging him to fly. This witness, in the French phrase, was a tall, portly man with a long black beard cut as if in the square pattern of his long black frock-coat, and having, somewhat incongruously, a monocle screwed into one eye. The last of the group, the second of the slayer's formal backers, stood motionless and somewhat apart from the rest—a big man, much younger than his comrades, and with a classical face like a statue's and almost as impassive as a statue's. By a movement common to the whole tragic company, he had removed his top-hat at the final announcement" (*The Man Who Knew Too Much*).

It is when we read such passages as this that we are reminded that their author began his career by being an artist. There is about the picture a singular and surprising clearness: the whole scene is vivid to the mind's eye. The *mind's* eye it is, however. In trying to analyse the impression it makes, one is driven onward into comparing it to that of a toy theatre, such as Chesterton loved all his life. Those beards, we feel, were stuck on; that gesture common to the whole company was as automatic as it was unanimous. Oddly enough, Chesterton seems to have felt the same:

"They followed his glance down to the garden by the wall, and the first thing they saw was that the rusty old garden door was standing open, letting in the white light of the road. Then they realized that a few yards within it was a tall, lean, grey-bearded man, clad completely in black and looking like some puritanic minister. He was standing on the turf looking down on the dead. A girl in grey, with a black hat, was kneeling by the body, and the two seconds had, as by an instinct of decency, withdrawn to some distance and stood gazing gloomily at the ground. *In the clear sunlight the whole group looked like a lighted scene on a green stage.*"

To point out the all but childishly simple way by which this effect has been achieved—the meticulous building up of the picture, item by item, with great regard for realism (the open gate would certainly have been seen before the people inside it); the rejection of all half-tones (as from "the white light of the road"); the characteristic repetitions—this is not in the least to disparage it. Such a style, individual chiefly through the absence of individuality, might profitably be copied by any apprentice to story-telling. But it is important to realize that it exhibits the simplicity of simplification, rather than that of simplicity itself. The world portrayed by Chesterton is not the real world, seen through the eyes of "second childhood", not even that of his own infancy, when men really wore beards and frock-coats, but a world of abstractions. It appeals neither to the senses nor to the imagination, but to the mind: it is poster-painted in words.

He could not turn words into a medium like light, which illuminates what it falls upon while remaining invisible itself: the spectrum of his own idiom was too diverting. The attraction of his most realistic tale lies not in its truth to life but in its style and moral He was, in fact, less of an artist than a dialectician. It is not the material of poetry—concrete objects, scenes and characters—that reflects his imaginative genius to the best advantage; it is the relatively abstract matter of philosophy.

§

Chesterton the philosopher is one of the most captivating, and at the same time one of the most bewildering writers in the world. To open any one of his books is to be caught, as securely as a fly in a spider's web—only rather more pleasantly. Imagine yourself, like a fly, entangled in a web. You are held by a mesh of interwoven threads, all glittering with dew-drops, all stretching far away to some end beyond your sight; you are aware of a pattern uniting them, but what it may be you have no idea. You try to free yourself. If you are impatient you begin by fluttering about, buzzing frantically—and find yourself all the more firmly held. Then you consider the best means of unravelling the knot. The first necessity is to find an end; and with that view you start following one of the threads that envelop you. But as with the threads composing a web, so with the strands of Chesterton's thought: if you want to find an end, you must needs wind all round the spiral until you reach the middle. Only when you have found that will you be able to break away—and the middle happens also to be the one place from which you may discern the pattern of the whole.

Chesterton spent a lifetime arguing (he said once that his occupation in life was "catching flies")[1]; he threw out his lines of argument in every direction: but he always threw them out from the same standpoint. It was the

[1] "On Thoughtless Remarks" in *All I Survey*.

standpoint of an imaginative vision. There is no direct communication of that vision in his works. What there is is an endless series of rationalizations of its component parts (the rationalization of the whole being thomist). If we wish to share the vision, therefore, we must follow the arguments; but we shall in all probability be unable to follow the arguments unless we share the vision, in some measure, already. "To him that hath shall be given, and from him that hath not shall be taken away, even that which he hath."

This is a paradox. But things discerned by the imagination can only be formulated, intellectually, by means of paradoxes. That is why Chesterton's own writing abounds in them. The body of his wit is paradoxical, because the soul of it is truth. That is why, also, some of his most brilliant epigrams were made to crystallize the views of other imaginative men, the most brilliant of them all to crystallize those of the most imaginative of them all; the marriage of wit and insight in his remark concerning Middleton Murry—"He is a voice crying in the wilderness, 'There is no God, and Marx is his prophet'"—was surely made in Heaven.

This is, in my opinion, the most perfect of Chesterton's paradoxes, because it is at once the most startling and the most searching. He saw things with both eyes—stereoscopically, so to speak; but his mastery of language is shown, not by his power of re-creating them before us, in all their concrete and complex simplicity—so that we too may perceive them as if for the first time—not by this, but by the rapidity with which he can expose them from the right and left by turns. Sometimes he does it so deftly that an illusion of direct seeing is obtained; and sometimes so fast that the illusion becomes truth. He presents a thesis, antithesis, and the mind combines them. Shaw, as he observed, is not paradoxical; wit of this kind, no less than humour, rests on an imaginative apprehension of the truth.

For what is, in fact, the essence of this paradox? One could go on trying to expound it for ever, and yet come no nearer to a definition. One might say that it involved a simultaneous denial of the God of anthropomorphic theology and reassertion of the God of experience: with an additional clause to the effect that Karl Marx was a vehicle of this God. But such an exposition would bring no conviction to those who know of no other God than the deity of anthropomorphic theology—whether they affirm his existence or deny it; and to those who do know the God of experience, it must appear for what it is—the clumsiest possible paraphrase for a perfect paradox.

Considering Chesterton's aversion to pantheism, it is rather surprising, when one comes to consider it, that he should have shown so much insight into Middleton Murry's creed. On other occasions, indeed, he resolutely refused to understand it. He refused to penetrate to the heart of what he called that "mystical paradox about losing freedom in order to be free" ("On Fate and a Communist" in *All I Survey*), which is Murry's answer to the problem of necessity and free will; he would not see that the pantheist who denied his charge, that "no special impulse to moral action" can possibly arise from a belief in absolute determinism, was asserting a contradiction neither more violent nor less defensible than he himself was doing, when he upheld "the complex God of the Athanasian Creed": and might indeed have used his own words to justify it—"This thing that bewilders the intellect utterly quiets the heart." The fallen angels were baffled by the problem, precisely because they were fallen angels—because they had lost the imagination, which is love. To the imagination it is self-evident that the pantheist contention is not a contradiction at all, but what

Chesterton actually called it, a paradox; that it involves, in other words, a simultaneous denial of one sort of free will and reassertion of another. Its illogic, like that of the Trinity, and of all the highest truths of high religion, is its most triumphant vindication.

For reality itself is illogical. Being a developing process, it is, and is not what it is, at any given moment. That process of denial in one mode and reassertion in another, which is the very heart of paradox, is also the very heart of all "becoming" or growth. That is why the thought that is loyal to it, formulated intellectually, can only be formulated in contradictions; the truth is always either self-evident or it is incomprehensible. It is self-evident to the imagination—and paradoxical; to the intellect it is incomprehensible—and a contradiction in terms. From the sublime to the ridiculous, all Chesterton's paradoxes may be cited in illustration of this fact. What does his reference to a man "proud of his humility" reflect, but the insight of a psychologist who knows the subtle and interminable process by which the *ego* arrogates to itself the virtue of the imagination or God? What does his demand that "the democracy be taught democracy" imply, but an analogous recognition of the negation of the spirit by the letter? Even his amusing words about the necessity of being unpractical involve the denial of one end in life and the reassertion of another. His wit and his philosophy are inseparable.

§

Chesterton's vision is imaginative, his expression of it intellectual. This is the central fact that explains nearly all the contradictions in his work. Not only the superficial and profound contradictions of his paradoxy, but the rather less amiable one, which repels many a serious reader, between the solemnity of the truth he is uttering and the overt vulgarity of its utterance.

This vulgarity of his—which, let it be said at once, is occasional only and has nothing to do with his gaiety—arises from an insensitiveness to the subtler emotional quality of words. He was insensitive to this in his own writing; and sometimes he proved himself unresponsive to it in the writing of others. In his own writing we find him indulging frequently in rhetoric. Now rhetoric is simply emotion become self-conscious, and is not by any means always a vice. The modern attitude of contempt towards it, at all times and in all circumstances, is an absurdity which should be dispelled by a single perusal of *Lepanto*. But the tawdry crescendoes that end one chapter after another of Chesterton's *Chaucer* can leave a very wry taste in our mouths. They are incongruous, and to a sensitive and interested reader they may be intolerable.

Equally incongruous are some of his references to the sayings of greater men than himself. When he dubs the sombre and magnificent paradox of Jesus, "He who loseth his life, the same shall save it", "not a piece of mysticism for saints and heroes, but a piece of everyday advice for sailors and mountaineers" (*Orthodoxy*)—we realize that there are moments when Chesterton "seems to debase and flatten everything he touches; and most of all when he touches worthy and exalted things" ("On Vulgarity" in *Come to Think of It*).

Fortunately these are not many. As we have suggested, to blame him for the hilarious incongruity of his similes in all his books would be to blame him for the chief strength of his style. It is just these that make him so vastly more readable and popular than almost any other writer of comparable significance. For if he did by his apparent flippancy drive away more than one serious (he would have said "solemn") seeker after truth, it is at least questionable whether they were not made up for by the hundreds who came to him for a laugh and stayed for the lesson. It is at least arguable whether his pamphlets were not as effective as the clarion-calls of the present *Weekly Review*, or even the audacious alarums and excursions of Mr. Pepler.

§

Moreover, between the highest form of art and mere artifice there are innumerable degrees; and in some of these Chesterton excelled all others. Mastery of language in any form, quite apart from subject-matter, may be considered artistry; and he was, indisputably, both one of the greatest essayists and one of the most successful humorous poets in our language.

Of Chesterton's light verse I will say little, except that it stands in a class by itself. The glorious fantasy of his best ballads was something new in English literature; nothing more riotously ironical than his songs for bank-clerks and post-office workers had ever been penned; nothing more sublimely crushing than the lines to F. E. Smith. His humour is not a sly smile, but a broad grin. All the features of his style which are defects in his more serious compositions—the tub-thumping rhythms, the glaring colours—are sources of strength to his humorous and satirical ones; and, as Mr. Julius West long ago pointed out (in *G. K. Chesterton: A Critical Study*. Secker, 1915), every advantage that the verse-form can offer, for sharpening antithesis or developing a refrain, Chesterton exploited to the utmost, with unerring felicity and inescapable effect.

But the essay was his literary form *par excellence*. Not only did he write more essays than anyone before or since;

he wrote better ones. Even if he had written nothing else but essays his works would still be impossible to read in their entirety; even if he had written nothing else, his place in English literature would be assured. More than any other writer of the first thirty years of this century, he kept alive the English tradition of essay-writing; and not only did he keep it alive—and what an achievement that was!—but he invented a new kind of writing which his essays exhibit to the best advantage. Paradox and irony, antithesis and a gentle humour, combine to produce a work of art, the distinctive quality of which can only be suggested by saying that, in some of the best examples, the manner of its presentation *is* the subject-matter.

Often it is said that Shaw's plays owe more in their structure to music than to literature. There is an analogy between the arrangement of Chesterton's early essays and that of some musical compositions. They remind one of Dohnani's "Nursery Suite", or Weinburger's variations on a familiar theme. "A series of paragraphs on some topical subject, with little spaces between them in order to encourage the weary reader"—so Julius West described them: but each paragraph is a new development of the original subject; and the reader is never weary. For the essay suited perfectly both Chesterton's temperament and his style. It must have appealed to his partiality for small things—even his longer discursive works, like *The Outline of Sanity* and *What's Wrong with the World*, tend to fall into a series of essays, just as his novels, like *The Man who Knew too Much* and *The Poet and the Lunatics*, fall into a series of short stories. And it suited his style because, in these longer works, however well it is sustained—*because* it is so well sustained—it palls or even insults. He who could be one of the most exhilarating, could also be one of the most exhausting of authors.

§

This introduces a much more serious charge against Chesterton's practice than his occasional vulgarity. It can and should be acknowledged that his wit was too exuberant. His parallels are too often real parallels, pursuing a course of their own independent of the main argument, which is all but lost sight of in their proliferation. Moreover, although he never indulged in paradoxes for their own sake, in the sense of striking them regardless of the truth, he did, very often, insert them where they were superfluous. In a writer less prodigal the compression into a single, arresting phrase of an argument that might take pages to unfold could only be looked upon as a virtue. But the reader of *Orthodoxy* knows a point of saturation, beyond which the mind calls out for a respite from epigrams. They no longer startle, only weary it. The writer alone seems never to have wearied. Towards the end of his life, he was still quite content to publish a book whose whole *raison d'être* seems to have been its paradoxes.

Reading *Four Faultless Felons* one cannot escape a suspicion that the title of the book was thought of first, suggesting in its turn the four sub-headings: "The Moderate Murderer", "The Honest Quack", "The Ecstatic Thief" and "The Loyal Traitor". The tales to fit these have been worked out with amazing ingenuity (though never, perhaps, with complete success). In each case the simple unfolding of a complicated plot, a detective story which is at the same time a paradox and a lively parable; the subtle interweaving of one *motif* with another, is carried out with a skill that cannot but command our admiration. Chesterton exactly described his method in such stories when he wrote of Shaw's plays that each is "an expanded epigram. But the epigram is not expanded (as with most people) into a hundred commonplaces. Rather the epigram is expanded into a hundred other epigrams; the work is at least as brilliant in detail as it is in design. But it is generally possible to discover the original and pivotal epigram which is the centre and purpose of the play" (*G. B. Shaw*). And yet, to measure the gulf that separates artifice from art, one has only to compare any one of these tales with one of his essays, or with an essay by Middleton Murry. The sheer subtlety of Murry's style, at its infrequent best, has seldom, if ever, been appreciated. It would be a bad sign if it were: for it exists as a means to an end, and not as an end in itself. In his "From the Lamb to the Bull" (as in Chesterton's "The Wind and the Trees", which is not one of those essays in which the manner is the matter) a multitude of threads of thought and feeling are woven into an organic unity so complete that such felicity, we feel, could never have been thought out: could only have come "as naturally as the leaves to a tree". Here the paradoxes of G. K. Chesterton startle us by their agility, Murry's astonish with their profundity. On this level there is all the difference between wit and wisdom, novelty and originality.

Novelty calls for mental acrobatics; originality demands a *katharsis*. Those who fancy it was the novelty of their technique that made the greatest of the Romantic poets and philosophers unpopular during their lives are far astray. They may seek to guard against the old error of Lockhart and Croker by an indiscriminating eulogy of everything unusual flaunting itself in the literary world to-day—they take for a resurrection the maggots heaving in the dead carcase of poetry. Mr. T. S. Eliot has more penetration than most of his following (which would be considerably reduced if it had to take his words seriously:

unfortunately, that is the necessity obviated by its own theory). Wordsworth, in his letter to Charles James Fox, Mr. Eliot writes, "proceeds to expound a doctrine which nowadays is called distributism", and in so doing,

> "He was not merely taking advantage of an opportunity to lecture a rather disreputable statesman and rouse him to useful activity; he was seriously explaining the purpose and content of his poems. . . . It is Wordsworth's social interest that inspires his own novelty of form in verse, and backs up his explicit remarks on poetic diction; and it is really this social interest which (consciously or not) the fuss was all about" (*The Use of Poetry and the Use of Criticism*).

Similarly Chesterton himself:

> ". . . the old quarrels were quarrels of quite a different sort. The motives of the attack on Keats were almost entirely political and social. The motives of the attack on Swinburne were almost entirely moral and religious. But it is not true, of either of these great poets, that they seemed utterly unreadable or unintelligible to those who had formed their taste on the older poets. Gifford was a low Tory hack, who hated and feared the little group of Radicals associated with Leigh Hunt and Shelley, and who regarded the very appearance of an apothecary's apprentice as a new poet in this group as a menacing sign of Jacobinism" ("On Mr. Epstein" in *Come to Think of It*).

The Romantics, even Keats, were hated because they were revolutionaries; and there is nothing men fear more than revolution, whether within themselves or without.

Few really great men have ever been popular except through a misunderstanding. Murry is out of fashion to-day principally because he has dared to tear away the trappings from men's heroes, and reveal them as heroic. Only when the astringent of the Romantic movement had been turned into a narcotic, its vision into a dream, did it become possible to represent Shelley's war on society as a passionate indictment of the stopped couplet.

Chesterton was misunderstood, with his own connivance. There are three ways of making a revolutionary innocuous; by making him a god, by calling him a genius and by turning him into "a character". The first is out of date; the second is wearing thin; the epoch of the third seems to have dawned. The last recorded act in the life of Adam Wayne, provost of Notting Hill, was the single-handed up-rooting of an oak-tree. After that he and King Auberon Quin set out through the world together in search of adventure: "Humour consists in the reversal of the obvious". In this sense, during forty years spent in almost unremitting reversal of the obvious, Chesterton uprooted a good many trees, and orchards too. In the end the occupation lost some of its original novelty in the eyes of the public. The crash of branches striking the ground became so familiar to men's ears, they scarcely bothered to turn round to see once again roots wriggling in the air, and the woodman contemplating his handi-work with the same quiet enjoyment as at first. They merely murmured to themselves smiling, "G.K. again", and continued on their daily round. So that, when the crashes abruptly stopped, and the woodman was no longer to be seen at his accustomed post, they found it hard to believe that the end of that great felling had really come, and that many rank growths were already bursting their pods and creeping up between the fallen trees.

Chesterton, who spent a lifetime preaching the necessity of seeing things as though they had never been seen before, lived to be one of the few features left on the landscape so well-known that it was unnoticed. The irony would have pleased him.

3

"To see the thing simply as it is, not as it is traditionally or conventionally supposed to be, is a gift of the 'daemonic' man, the creative spirit. . . . The fresh, direct and uncorrupted view of the situation, whether in science, or art, or history, or politics is the privilege of the 'daemonic' man. . . . Thus the 'daemonic' is essentially revolutionary in appearance, in whatever province of human activity it manifests itself" (J. Middleton Murry, "Heaven and Earth").

To one approaching Chesterton's works for the first time, perhaps the most striking thing about them is the versatility they display. There seems, at first sight, to be only one province of human activity with which he was unconcerned, and that was science. He was, as a matter of fact, always inclined to be less than just to both science and scientists. It is possible that he was no more able than his friend to recognize the vision he preached when it expressed itself through facts and figures: though this failure is curious when we remember the nature of his insight elsewhere.

In one of the first of his poems, which, he said, contained the "foundation of the philosophy of his later years", there occurs the following verse:

" The sun was black with judgement, and the moon
    Blood, but between
I saw a man stand, saying, 'To me at least
    The grass is green'."[1]

Now it is perfectly true, as D. H. Lawrence declared, that a child, when it cries, "Why is the grass green?" is not enquiring but exclaiming; and they are dull pedants

[1] "Femina contra Mundum" in *The Wild Knight*, see note to 2nd edn.

who seize on the pretext for prating about chlorophyll. But when a naturalist says, "Why is the grass green?" he is both exclaiming and enquiring. Admittedly the exclamatory element is often lost sight of. There is a type of scientist (usually conspicuous at meetings of the British Association) who regards everything explained as something explained away. Often he is the same who looks upon some acquaintance with pachyderms or plankton as a passport to theology: and Chesterton held him, justly, in low esteem. The greatest scientists, however, from Aristotle to Freud, have not been of this breed. Darwin might have described his sublime synthesis of a thousand minute and loving observations[1] in the very words used by Chesterton of his conversion to Christian orthodoxy. And so might Freud; for the dynamic of psycho-analysis derives from Freud's seeing as apparent miracles, demanding explanation, a host of phenomena which all others had taken as matters of course.

Chesterton left science to the scientists. But he wrote plays and novels, poems and detective-stories, pamphlets, proclamations and epistles on every subject under the sun, and some over it. He was not a great playwright, novelist or poet, nor a supreme master of the short story: but he was never a dull one; and he did succeed in doing what very few writers since Dickens or Stevenson have done—he created a character lively enough to roam beyond the wide circle of his own readers. Nor can there be much doubt who was the spiritual ancestor of Father Brown: "The round, moon-like face and round, moon-like spectacles of Samuel Pickwick . . . move

---

[1] *Cf., Reminiscences of my Father's Everyday Life*, by Sir Francis Darwin (Watts, 1929): "Thus in the *Origin*, p. 440, there is a description of a larval cirripede, 'with six pairs of beautifully constructed natatory legs, a pair of magnificent compound eyes, and extremely complex antennae'. We used to laugh at him for this sentence, which we compared to an advertisement."

through the tales as emblems of a certain spherical simplicity. They are fixed in that grave surprise that may be seen in babies; that grave surprise that is the only real happiness that is possible to man" (*Dickens*).

§

The art at which Chesterton excelled was literary criticism. In calling criticism an art we are, of course, using the term 'art' in a broader sense than is customary, and perhaps too broad. Criticism is really a halfway house between art and philosophy: that is why so many social and political philosophers have begun their careers as critics. Nevertheless, the affinity between art and criticism is very close: how close Chesterton himself revealed in the casual phrase, "After all, what we want is direct and individual impressions of primary objects, *whether poets or pine-trees*" ("On the Standardization of Stevenson" in *All I Survey*). Literary criticism demands of its exponent a readiness for self-obliteration of exactly the same quality as poetry or painting: not merely a "willing suspension of disbelief", but a suspension of belief. The critic approaching his object must be able to make a holocaust at once of conventional prejudice and the more intimate bias of his own convictions, if he is to approach it imaginatively, from within outwards. His mind must be a "thoroughfare for all thoughts"; his reason and sensibility alike on tip-toe for their quarry—"that strangeness of things which is the light in all poetry, and indeed in all art" (*St. Thomas Aquinas*), otherwise his appraisement will stop short at externals, attentive only to the logical content of the lines, or else become, like much of Swinburne's, a thing that is neither prose nor poetry, appreciation nor exposition. Chesterton's studies, with a few significant exceptions, such as his

Blake, are always of this character. And of course they are saturated through and through with his own peculiar and Christian humour. It may be confidently asserted that only a great critic could have composed his parodies on Tennyson and Walt Whitman.

OLD KING COLE

Me clairvoyant,
Me conscious of you, old camarado,
Needing no telescope, lorgnette, field-glass, opera-glass,
  myopic pince-nez,
Me piercing two thousand years with eye naked and not
  ashamed;
The crown cannot hide you from me;
Musty old feudal-heraldic trappings cannot hide you from
  me,
I perceive that you drink.
(I am drinking with you. I am as drunk as you are).
I see you are inhaling tobacco, puffing, smoking, spitting
(I do not object to your spitting).
You prophetic of American largeness,
You anticipating the broad masculine manners of these
  States,
I see in you also there are movements, tremors, tears,
  desire for the melodious;
I salute your three violinists, endlessly making vibrations,
Rigid, relentless, capable of going on for ever;
They play my accompaniment; but I shall take no notice
  of any accompaniment;
I myself am a complete orchestra.
So long.

Chesterton never came nearer than that to direct revelation. That *is* Whitman, seen with the understanding that is love, and the love that is laughter. The same insight characterizes his studies of Stevenson, Dickens and Chaucer.

Because his criticism is of this quality, deriving from an imaginative apprehension of primary objects, it avoids all classifications. Delighting in diversity, Chesterton had no hankering after the specious uniformity imposed by such terms as "classical" and "romantic". He was free to acknowledge that there are as many different kinds of poetry as there are poets, and to enjoy each for its own merits. These terms are useful within limits, so long as they are kept as classifications. But they are for ever being turned into judgements, by one party or another, because they are for ever being used by men of one idea—"single-eyed" intellectuals. The Romantic poets descended to this level, when they denounced the eighteenth century for not conforming to their own, quite inapplicable canons; the self-styled "classicists" of the present day do likewise, only with less excuse. Few of them thank G. K. Chesterton for the first effort of this century towards a rehabilitation of Pope. "Judge not that ye be not judged": refusing classifications, he became unclassifiable himself.

A critic more in vogue to-day than Chesterton ever was accustomed himself and his readers to drawing a hard and fast distinction between the formlessness, the dreamy sensuality of Romantic art, and the purpose, unity and decorum of the Classical masters. The most remarkable thing about this antithesis is that the late eighteenth and early nineteenth centuries themselves were quite unconscious of its existence. For the essence of the Classic spirit Mr. Irving Babbitt saw exemplified, not in the Italians of the Renaissance, the followers of Daniello, nor the Romans, their models, but the Greeks; yet they, so far from being spurned by the Romantics with a characteristic immoderation, as we should expect if his hypothesis were true, held a positive fascination for them. In Germany, indeed, as Miss Butler has recently shown (E. M. Butler: *The Tyranny of Greece over Germany*), it amounted to nothing less than a tyranny; for not until it had claimed for tribute the poetic life of the unhappy Hölderlin did a Theseus arise strong enough to vanquish it. Heine broke the spell and banished the gods from Olympus: Hermes to a ferry-boat, Bacchus to a monastery, and Zeus to an Arctic *igloo*. In England, however, even so esoteric a genius as Blake conceived it as his mission to "renew the lost art of the Greeks"; Keats prayed for the "old vigour" of their bards; and to Shelley, who welcomed the Greek war of independence with a drama modelled on Aeschylus, it appeared that "no other epoch in the history of our species" had left "fragments stamped so visibly with the image of the divinity in man". To Babbitt all this was but one more illustration of the Romantic nostalgia—and "nostalgia I have defined as the pursuit of pure illusion". Yet it was at least as much Greek art as the isles of Greece that these poets revered, as their words show, and Babbitt would hardly have called the Hermes of Praxiteles a "pure illusion". Did it never seem to him strange that, with every period and place in history at their disposal, these "aimless and lawless" Romantics, these sensual rebels against "all the formal boundaries and limits that the past had set up", should have chosen classical Greece for their Arcadia? (*Cf.*, I. Babbitt: *The New Laocoon* and *Rousseau and Romanticism.*)

The truth is that the familiar distinction has no significance at a certain level: and to that level Chesterton by imagination belonged. From the one side he was deprecated as "romantic", because of his fondness for the colourful and Catholic middle ages; from the other rated as "classical" since he accepted the external discipline of a church. He was neither, and both. Eventually Rousseauists and neo-classicists alike solved the problem of his position in English letters by leaving him out of their histories altogether. He, however, had room for them in his superior vision even when they had none for him in their classifications. The wise words of Lord Hugh Cecil, which Chesterton quoted in his autobiography, have a wider application than to *Orthodoxy* and its critics: "Truth can understand error, but error cannot understand truth."[1]

§

It would, we feel, be faintly extravagant to speak of G. K. Chesterton as a "daemonic" spirit, or even to refer to his vision as "daemonic": there is too much of high seriousness implied in that term. It would, however, be still more extravagant to deny that his vision had much in common with that of the "daemonic" man. Like his, it was direct and uncorrupted; and like his, it was revolutionary—or it would have been, if ever it had been heeded.

In studying Chesterton it is always necessary to remember that he became both a revolutionary and a Roman Catholic long before it was the fashion among the intelligentsia to be either. Either, but seldom both. His own revolutionism, no less than his Christianity, sustained itself from a real contact with real things. With the Communism and Catholicism of intellectuals he can have had but little sympathy: both being based on abstractions. The Marxian proletariat is an abstraction; and so is the Kingdom of Heaven that is within men and yet seeks no revolutionary embodiment in the social system of

[1] An aphorism which aptly summarizes the chapter in *Orthodoxy* itself entitled "The Maniac".

which they are a part. For it is as true that there is no individual apart from society as it is that there is no society apart from its individual members. It is curious, as well as significant, that Marxists are seldom paradoxical. At the very heart of their philosophy lies the truth that reality, being a developing process, cannot be apprehended logically, only dialectically. Yet their philosophy can have no vital meaning for them. Perhaps if it did they would cease to be intellectuals. It is accepted blindly, as theirs is accepted by the Catholic intellectuals; and therefore any suggestion that the two systems, understood in the spirit, would cease to negate one another, converge and be confirmed in a higher synthesis is, though dialectical to the depths, regarded with abhorrence by both.

It was, however, for just such a synthesis that Chesterton stood. His profound saying, that "until we love a thing in all its ugliness we cannot make it beautiful" is naturally complemented in the realm of politics by his contention that a revolutionary movement, to be successful, must be inspired by the rights of man and not downcast by his wrongs. He understood and disclosed thirty years ago, far more nakedly than the dialectical materialists of the present day, the true connection between art and politics. He understood that the dynamic of each, when it is dynamic, springs from an identical imaginative vision. The self-forgetful contemplation of the artist, the Christian reverence for the individual, is the "democratic emotion" of the true revolutionary.

> "The thing which is really required for the proper working of democracy is not merely the democratic system, or even the democratic philosophy, but the democratic emotion. . . . It is a certain instinctive attitude which feels the things in which men all agree

to be unspeakably important, and all the things in which they differ (such as mere brains) to be almost unspeakably unimportant" (*Heretics*).

It is not irrelevant to point out that Chesterton would certainly have condemned that last sentence had it been uttered by a Buddhist or pantheist. Much more important is it, however, to grasp his meaning firmly with all its implications, for this is a truth that has repeatedly, and fatally, been lost sight of since the war of 1914–18.

"Democracy is not philanthropy; it is not even altruism or social reform. Democracy is not founded on pity for the common man; democracy is founded on reverence for the common man, or, if you will, even on fear of him. It does not champion man because man is so miserable, but because man is so sublime. It does not object so much to the ordinary man being a slave as to his not being a king, for its dream is always the dream of the first Roman republic, a nation of kings" (*op. cit.*).

In the epilogue to his brilliant book *Plato To-day*, Mr. R. H. S. Crossman reaches the same conclusion, with a different emphasis. "True democracy", he says, "is un-Platonic, because it springs from the Christian notion of personality"; and "as the true democrat must start with the assumption that the world has still to be made democratic, so the Christian must assume that it is still pagan, despite the existence of 'democratic' institutions and 'Christian' churches". For fundamentally both Christianity and democracy are assertions of incredibles: "Against the realism of those who accept the existing order and seek to maintain it, they preach an impossibility and try to make it come true."

In this perspective lies the true notion of the equality of man, which is not a mechanical but a mystical conception. Equality, in the eyes and on the lips of its first great champions, never meant equality in "mere brains" or talent, any more than in physique; nor can it be exorcized (as Professor Haldane and others suppose) by disproving these claims that were never made. The equality of men resides in something far more fundamental than these, something allied to that beauty beyond beauty which the artist reveals even in ugly things—a universal dignity manifest to an all-comprehending love. The philosophy that can provide a foundation for democracy must be one that has room in it for this love—which is only another name for "the democratic emotion"; no other will suffice: and such a philosophy will necessarily involve a theology, for this love is all that men really know of God.

This was Chesterton's consistent reply to those who, like Father John O'Connor, assailed the doctrine of the equality of men on the ground that it was illogical: "true equality was a mystical fact, only divinely revealed, that all men are equal only in the sight of God" (O'Connor: *Father Brown on G. K. Chesterton*). In one of his essays he points out how faith in democracy and faith in God have declined concurrently in the western world:

> "All men are equal because God loves all equally: and nothing can compare with that equality. But in what other way are men equal? The vague Liberals of the nineteenth century cut away the divine ground from under democracy, and democracy was left to stand by itself. In other words, it is left to fall by itself. Jefferson said that men were given equal rights by their Creator. Ingersoll said they had no Creator, but had received equal rights from nowhere. Even in the

democratic atmosphere of America, it began to dawn on a great many people that it is very difficult to prove that men ever received the equal rights at all" ("On Romanticism and Youth" in *All I Survey*).

It was another example of the world's "using, and using up, the truths that remain to it out of the old treasury of Christendom". But, as before, we need not agree with Chesterton that the only way to arrest this deterioration is by returning to a full profession of Christianity. The way to arrest it is by advancing to an equally comprehensive pantheism. For, after all, it is not a transcendental, but an immanent God whom men participate in and perceive, when they acknowledge the divine particularity of the world.

The democratic emotion aspires naturally to its embodiment in a society of human brotherhood: which means a society of universal spontaneity, for brotherhood is love, and love can only be spontaneous. Such a society is what most of the great democrats have meant by "democracy" itself; and, with the vision of it clearly before their eyes, they have known how to value existing institutions. They have revered the "democratic system" because it reflects an approximation (however remote) to the ideal, inasmuch as toleration, whether of religious or political opinion, finds expression in its laws; and trust, which is allied to toleration, in its constitution. Those who ridicule democracy, ridicule toleration; and those who ridicule toleration, ridicule love, of which it is an essential component. Therefore respect for what has been achieved, no less than ambition for what has not, characterize the true democrat in a "democratic" society. Chesterton was a liberal before he became a socialist.

§

Naturally, he rejected the "economic interpretation of history". For that theory, as it is understood by most of its exponents, rests on the abstraction of one element from the complex whole of history, and its promotion to a position of absolute responsibility for all the rest. Chesterton had no use for such abstractions. The faculty that can grasp only one aspect of a phenomenon at a time—the continuity, but not the diversity of the colours in a spectrum—Bergson calls the "intellect". Most socialist theoreticians are intellectuals. They suffer, as Chesterton thought the Arab metaphysicians suffered, from "a lack of the vitality that comes from complexity, and of the complexity that comes from comparison" (*The New Jerusalem*). To the power that can grasp all at once Bergson assigns the name of "intuition". Chesterton had intuition—which is also direct perception. For the economic determinist there are but two paths open at this moment of history: to co-operate in the automatic development of productive technique, or be superannuated. He cannot admit the possibility of reversing it, because the denial of any effective reality to the individual as such is knit into the very fabric of the theory of Marxist Socialism.

Chesterton's criticism of economic determinism was the same as his criticism of every other sort of determinism. It was that propounded in the *St. Thomas Aquinas*:

"The mind is not merely receptive, in the sense that it absorbs sensations like so much blotting-paper; on that sort of softness has been based all that cowardly materialism which conceives man as wholly servile to his environment. On the other hand, the mind is not purely creative, in the sense that it paints pictures on the windows and then mistakes them for the landscape outside. But the mind is active. . . ."

He said of Bolshevism that it did not "seek to establish a complete philosophy such as Aquinas founded on Aristotle". This is true. Marxism, in its crude Russian form, which is the form most widely popularized in this country, has no place in it either for Marx or Lenin, except in the capacity of undistinguishable economic units. Chesterton's criticism is, however, inadequate when applied to the early philosophy of Marx himself. In the third of the *Theses on Feuerbach* occur the following words:

> "The materialistic teaching that human beings are the products of circumstance and education, and changed human beings the products of changed circumstances and education, leaves out of count the fact that circumstances themselves are changed by human beings; that the educator must himself be educated."

It was this young Marx also who uttered the maxim to which Chesterton is at this moment giving so perfect an illustration, "The criticism of religion is the necessary pre-condition of all criticism". It is the teaching of the later, messianic prophet that needs to be completed by another, less famous dictum, from *The New Jerusalem* (significant title): that self-criticism is the necessary condition of all criticism.

> "A thing like the Catholic system is a system; that is, one idea balances and corrects another. A man like Mohammed or Marx, or in his own way Calvin, finds

that system too complex, and simplifies everything to a single idea. . . . He naturally builds a rather unbalanced system with his one definite idea" ("On the Open Conspiracy" in *Come to Think of It*).

Marx-Leninism, by excluding the democratic emotion, ultimately excludes the democratic ideal. A book which gained considerable notoriety in 1937 was called *The Road to Wigan Pier*. It was by a socialist, George Orwell, and purported to be an accurate portrayal of the condition of the working class in Great Britain. Probably it was accurate, though there was something in the tone of the book which offended more than one working-class reader, in a way in which Chesterton's pamphlets never did. What is of more importance in this connection is that this author faced up to the prospects which an unlimited expansion of mechanical technique involves. Socialists, as Chesterton remarked in *The Outline of Sanity*, are not fond of looking at their utopia closely. The only important exception is William Morris, and his England of the twenty-second century bears a near resemblance to that of the fourteenth: a fact which a modern communist finds "irritating".[1] George Orwell does, however, glance into the future—only to avoid drawing the logical conclusions from his material. Finding that the prospect is anything but alluring, he turns hurriedly away, with the observation that the time has not yet come for such speculations; the social ownership of the means of production must be established. The time has not come to decide what is desirable; our duty is to desire it.

Chesterton began his original development where the modern socialist leaves off. He understood the economic

[1] J. Strachey: *The Theory and Practice of Socialism*, (Gollancz, 1936). "Morris's mediaevalism and his generally anti-scientific attitude may make some parts of his account of a communist Britain irritating to-day."

element in history as well as most; he recognized also the moral, or human: and this he believed to be determinant. The supreme factor was not "the bodily framework, or the framework of environment, but the frame of mind" ("On Suicide, North and South" in *All I Survey*). Development of productive methods gave the opportunities for new approximations to the ideal; it did not automatically give rise to the morality capable of making use of them. He was, in fact, a "possibilist". History, as Edward Carpenter remarked, is a difficult horse to ride; but the possibility of curbing it admitted, the necessity of a moral dynamic to that end propounded, and Chesterton at least was proof against the absurdities of those who, whether "bourgeois" or anti-bourgeois, "talk about Efficiency without any criticism of Effect" (*The Thing*).

Once again, there was nothing essentially new in his criticism of the Marxist socialist viewpoint. As early as *Orthodoxy* itself he had written:

> "We have said we must be fond of this world, even in order to change it. Now we add that we must be fond of another world (real or imaginary) in order to have something to change it to. . . . Progress should mean that we are always changing the world to suit the vision. Progress does mean (just now) that we are always changing the vision."

§

He himself was fond of another world, and it was partly real and partly imaginary. His ideal was, of course, the democratic ideal—a society of human brotherhood. But he believed such a society to have been more nearly approached at a certain period in the past than it is anywhere in the world to-day. The men who followed Constantine, he said, passed through the tunnel of the dark ages and "came out into a world more wonderful than the eyes of men have looked on before or after; they heard the hammers of hundreds of happy craftsmen working for once according to their own will, and saw St. Francis walking with his halo a cloud of birds" (*The New Jerusalem*).

By this vision Chesterton is triply assimilated to the great prophets of the Romantic movement. Again and again his drum and fife are to be heard where their organ sounded, playing the identical tune. Rousseau himself had made the child the focus of his philosophy: "the age at which the individual man would like to stop" is the starting-point for his consideration of the "natural man" (that combination or confusion of our "natural" and Goethe's *Natur*); all the Romantics had been ardent classicists; and what the older of them (the *ältere Romantik* of Germany) had seen in Greece, the younger had discovered in the middle ages also.

Like the medievalism of the Romantics, Chesterton's was, and still is, often derided, or else laughed at as though it consisted of nothing but a fondness for bugles and bright colours. It is, however, fundamental to all his thinking; and it illustrates the constructive side of both his historical and political criticism. In a sense he regarded the medieval as the norm of a human society. It was the same sense in which a gardener may regard the full-blown rose as the norm, even though flowers stunted by frost or starved by bad soil may be much more common. He saw in it a society of men all of whose faculties were constantly employed to the full.

"The peasant does live, not merely a simple life, but a complete life." He is always in touch with real, individual things, that keep alive both his senses and his imagination; he is never in danger of mistaking the abstractions of the intellect for the particularities of experience. Similarly the craftsman: in the middle ages he was not starved of his creative satisfaction, as the modern factory-operative is, who spends his life turning a single wheel or screw. Chesterton believed that both peasant and craftsman, moreover, felt themselves to be parts of an organic whole: indeed, without the security and demand which that sense gave him, the craftsman would never have achieved what he did. In medieval, as in Greek society, men were not aware, as they are now, of an "immense distance between the craftsman and the crowd". If they had been, "they would never have set the craftsman to work solely for the crowd. In that case there would never have been any such trifles as the Parthenon or the cathedral of Seville" ("On Mr. Epstein" in *Come to Think of It*).

To those who accused him of "escaping from reality into the past" (as if "reality" were confined to factories and films and newspapers) Chesterton might have retorted that there was, in a very real sense, *more* reality in the life of a medieval villager than in that of the average modern townsman. His medievalism, like William Morris's own, was the longing for a society in which the human relation between man and nature, and between man and man, had never been obscured by the intermediacy of machinery and the "cash-nexus". The mention of these things, however, recalls a difference between their cult of the middle ages and that of the other great Romantics to whom we have referred. Chesterton and Morris were not philosophical idealists; they both realized that the economic bases of society would have to be changed before their ideal could become a reality.

§

"Ideal" is perhaps the wrong word, if it is taken to refer to the middle ages themselves. Chesterton's ideal society was based upon the medieval, but based upon it, like M. Maritain's, according to the *analogical* principle of Aquinas; he did not desire a return to the past. Nor did he ever overestimate the happiness of the hundreds of craftsmen, though the passage quoted above from *The New Jerusalem*, taken by itself, would suggest that. "Men with medieval sympathies are sometimes accused, absurdly enough, of trying to prove that the medieval period was perfect. In truth the whole case for it is that it was imperfect." "It is bound up with the quality of the civilization in question that it was potential rather than perfect; and there is no need to idealize it in order to regret it." He had more historical imagination than most of his critics, more of that "historical humility" without which, as he said, "no great works will seem great, and no wonders of the world will seem wonderful" (*The New Jerusalem*).

Agreeing with Rousseau (of whom he wrote one of the few sensible criticisms that have appeared in the last twenty years) that "democracy is never quite democratic except when it is quite direct; and it is never quite direct except when it is quite small", he could appreciate the real virtues of the village-community, including the sense of mutual responsibility which it involved. But he believed that it might have developed into something far finer, combining with these the positive elements of individualism. "As a fact, of course, this system throughout Christendom was already evolving into a pure peasant proprietorship; and it will be long before industrialism evolves into anything so equal and so free." All that had been required was a disinterested party prepared to make it its duty to safeguard the right of the peasants, at the time when the feudal system was decaying. But the Church, which was committed by its teaching to such a course, and alone had the authority to enforce it, joined hands with the oppressors, exploited the peasantry itself, and failed to set its face determinedly against usury while its determination might yet have prevailed. The irresponsible element of individualism got the upper hand, and it has held it to the present day. This was what Chesterton believed; he could believe it only by rejecting the theory of economic determinism. For him it was not inevitable that the Church should have betrayed its trust. Had its morale not been sapped by the Black Death and the failure of the Crusades it might have done otherwise, and the evils of competitive industrialism have been spared. By the development of the powers of production a choice had been set before men, and they had chosen wrongly. It might have been turned to the advantage of the whole community, and was made use of for the enrichment of the few. "Medievalism died, but it died young."

And now, Chesterton believed, the wheel had turned full circle, and another choice was being set before men, by the development of competitive industrialism itself. The historical imagination which had played upon the past he turned upon the present also; and this was the greater achievement. For objectivity towards the present means objectivity with regard to one's own interests; means, in fact, an impassioned disinterestedness. Chesterton's evolution from Liberalism into Socialism was perfectly natural. He saw that the work of the former had been accomplished, when equal political rights were accorded to all men. The democratic emotion must find a new outlet; it found it in Socialism.

"We have now to assume not only that all citizens are equal, but that all men are citizens. Capitalism attempted it by combining political equality with economic inequality; it assumed that the rich would always hire the poor. But Capitalism seems to me to have collapsed; to be not only a discredited ethic but a bankrupt business" (*op. cit.*).

This was written after he had come to call himself a distributist. But Chesterton "saw our industrial civilization as rooted in injustice long before it became so common a comment as it is to-day" (*Autobiography*). The truth and courage of his revolutionary vision were never more surely demonstrated than in his refusal to take even usury for granted. But because he was aware that direct seeing had been demanded of him at his own cost—it is not comfortable nowadays to realize that the acts we perform as social units are no less our own than our personal relationships—he was proof from the first against the deception of socialist caricature. What he beheld was not the calculated exploitation of one class by another, but an all-pervading injustice accepted as a matter of course nearly as much by the "proletarian" as the capitalist. What he strove to create was a general consciousness of its existence, equal to his own, so that it must either become deliberate and challenging, or else be rectified, by the substitution of co-operation for competition.

The fundamental socialist demand for the communal ownership of industry Chesterton never relinquished. He was not such a medievalist as to believe in a total abolition of factories; and it is important to realize that his Distributism was in no sense a going back on his Socialism. He never went back on anything. All that was of positive value in Socialism he incorporated in the distributist programme. Where he differed from most socialists was in the genuineness of his belief in "turning the inventions of the age of machinery to the benefit of the community as a whole". He understood men; and thereby knew what actually was to their benefit, and what to their ultimate dehumanization. "Instead of the machine being a giant to which man is a pigmy, we must at least reverse the proportions until man is a giant to whom the machine is a toy" (*The Outline of Sanity*). In fact he was in a position not unlike that of the solitary professor in *Erewhon*, who suggested that the machine might be regarded as an appendage to mankind, instead of mankind as an appendage to the machine; only whereas the latter theory was, very logically, made a pretext for the destruction of machinery by the Erewhonians, by the modern socialist it is used as an argument for its retention. The professor in the story was not listened to by many, and nor was Chesterton.

Commerce was made for man, and not man for commerce. Chesterton was never tired of upholding this thesis. It is the dominant theme of the whole of one of his most masterly works, *What's Wrong with the World*. In fact its contrary *was* what he believed to be wrong.

> "This is the huge modern heresy of altering the human soul to fit its conditions, instead of altering human conditions to fit the human soul. If soap-boiling is really inconsistent with brotherhood, so much the worse for soap-boiling, not for brotherhood. If civilization really cannot get on with democracy, so much the worse for civilization, not for democracy. Certainly, it would be far better to go back to village communes, if they really are communes. Certainly, it would be better to do without soap rather than to do without society. Certainly, we would sacrifice all our wires,

wheels, systems, specialities, physical science and frenzied finance for one half-hour of happiness such as has often come to us with comrades in a common tavern. I do not say the sacrifice will be necessary; I only say it will be easy."

From the beginning to the end of his career he laboured this point, on one pretext after another; contemporary England did not leave him in want of pretexts. Towards the end, indeed, he seems at times to have become almost obsessed with it. Some of the initial buoyancy and freshness are absent from his later essays; a note of angry reiteration creeps into them; and I am told that the same note became apparent in his conversation. But we should not find fault with him for this. Rather it is a tribute to his sense of the paramount, crying evil of our time and nation: for, as Mr. R. H. Tawney has declared, industrialism in England is a national vice, equivalent to, and not less sordid than, the militarism of Hohenzollern Prussia.

The problem with which he was grappling was the same as would confront an honest Socialism in this country: namely, how to reconcile the value of individual liberty, which has been the positive contribution of the age of individualism, with that sense of social responsibility which vanished with the village commune. He was not insensitive to the difficulties involved. The whole atmosphere of a mechanized society, with its depersonalized mode of living, is hostile even to the preservation of such true democracy as exists, let alone to its extension on the economic plane. It is more hostile to the establishment of Socialism than the village commune itself would have been:

"Feudal manorial life was not a democracy; but it could have been much more easily turned into a democracy. Later peasant life, as in France or Switzerland, actually has been quite easily turned into a democracy. But it is horribly hard to turn what is called modern industrial democracy into a democracy" ("On Industrialism" in *All I Survey*).

Nevertheless, Chesterton had hope: because he believed that the wish for security, and not ambition for superior wealth, was really the abiding motive of the human heart. This he revered, and this he trusted. It was by virtue of this that he was enabled to believe in the restoration of a peasantry to England, not collectivized like the Russian, but independent like the French.

§

It is an attractive ideal, the distributist—the most attractive political ideal known to me. And it is not in the least utopian; it depends, for its realization, on no impossible change in human nature as we know it. As it was expounded by Chesterton, indeed, the distributist ideal is almost identical, in its main features, with that *idéal historique* which another thomist, M. Maritain, has sketched, and which he distinguishes absolutely from the *idéal utopique* (*Cf.* Maritain: *Humanisme Intégral*). Nor has it anything in common with totalitarianism, though it is often enough labelled fascistic or reactionary by muddled left-wing thinkers. The very title, "Distributism" is the antithesis of "totalitarianism"; and this antithesis is maintained on every level of its programme, economic, political and religious. Only those who are so ignorant as to call Fascism (that utterly modern manifestation) a "return to the middle ages", and imagine that they are thereby insulting it, could confuse with it the Distributist Commonwealth.

Chesterton, like Maritain, believed that the centralization of large-scale industry, its communal, co-operative or state control, was natural and desirable; but he was not, as most communists are, bemused by the abstract idea of collectivism; he regarded the decentralization of agriculture as no less natural and desirable. He looked, moreover, for a vast multiplication of small stores—a nation of shop-keepers. Totalitarianism betrays its urban origin at once in its drive for collectivism in industry, where it is inevitable and beneficent, and its incapacity even to imagine an humane individual proprietorship. In its fascistic guise it appeals to the desperate shop-keeper—he who is being crushed between the pincers of monopoly capitalism and the menace of Communism—but it appeals to him only to betray him: for it cannot grasp the idea, or ideal, of a unity in diversity. Its agent is the intellect—the only faculty left unatrophied in a mechanized society; and the only unity the intellect can grasp is a uniformity—in this case the uniformity of collectivism.

As on the economic, so on the political level: it is uniformity that totalitarianism aims at. The changes it brings about, the liquidation of vast anti-social interests, the organization of a nation for aggression or defence, may demand intolerant methods; but intolerance itself can be exercised only upon an abstraction, whether it be called the class or the race. And here also Distributism confronts it in an attitude of defiance: for Distributism is democratic through and through; it springs from the imagination which includes the intellect. Moreover, because it is imaginative, it is truly religious; and because it is truly religious, it is truly catholic. That deification of the exclusive state, which is the religion of totalitarianism, is utterly repugnant to it.

It is catholic, but it is not necessarily Roman Catholic.

Chesterton was beyond sectarianism when he became a distributist. When he called on volunteers to begin the good work of restoring an independent peasantry, he knew that only the imaginative would respond: for they alone would appreciate the necessity of re-personalizing social relationships; and the imagination can be trusted, in whatever forms it may express itself. (No doubt he thought that it could be trusted to express itself ultimately in his own form also—but that is a different matter).

The campaign which occupied the later years of his life had for its aim this restoration, to be accomplished by the road of moral resolution, lest it be compelled along the road of ruin.

> "I think it is not unlikely that in any case a simpler social life will return; even if it return by the road of ruin. I think the soul will find simplicity again, if it be in the Dark Ages. But we are Christians and concerned with the body as well as the soul; we are Englishmen and we do not desire, if we can help it, that the English people should be merely the People of the Ruins."

The Outline of Sanity, in many respects his most perfect book[1]—the one in which his humour and insight are most exquisitely balanced and blended—was published in 1926, the year of the general strike; and it is clear from the context that Chesterton was thinking, when he wrote these words, of an internal collapse of the nation. He accepted the Marxian diagnosis of the contraditions in capitalist economy. In fact he used the concentration of capital in progressively fewer and fewer hands as a text for turning their own ideology against the capitalists. He pointed out, as ever, what those who saw things only as their fathers

---

[1] The most perfect of his books in all respects seems to me to be his *St. Francis*.

has seen them altogether failed to perceive: that it was equally ridiculous either to defend or attack modern "capitalism" on the ground that it was competitive, when the whole trend of the system was towards the extirpation of competition through the growth of monopolies. He pointed out that private property itself was already almost a thing of the past: "The same industrial individualism which set out with no thought except private property has produced a new world in which private property is hardly ever thought of, or at least not primarily as private" ("On Education" in *All I Survey*). Emperor and spectators alike were disgraced by the voice of a little child, crying, "But he has no clothes on!"

The collapse he foresaw, however, has not come to pass. Instead, in the two countries from whose circumstances Marxists would have predicted, and did most confidently predict, upheaval, an unprecedented degree of economic and political integration has been achieved: integration totally focused upon international war. Of the fascist states, those incarnations of abstractionism, what had Chesterton to say? "I do not think much of Hitler's funny little crooked cross, and his ranting and romantic quotations from Nietzsche, yet there is a great deal to be said for poor old Hitler. It is part of a great movement for return of order to human government" (G.K.C. reported in *The Morning Post*, May 25, 1933). Even in the political realm his "character" obtruded, challenging people not to take him seriously and clouding over his real democratic vision. Nor can it, I think, be denied that his Roman Catholicism perverted his judgement of political events. He was right in insisting on the divergencies that exist between Nazism and Italian Fascism; still more in pointing out to those who would damn both with the one facile adjective "undemocratic" that an authoritarian régime of one kind or another may at times be the only alternative to anarchy that faces a country. Yet only the concordat between Mussolini and the Holy See can have led Chesterton to overlook the Duce's deliberate and avowed subordination of the human personality to the state, and to condone the brutal invasion of Abyssinia.

There was, however, a deeper reason that this for his failure to start a dynamic political movement. The internal collapse which he predicted has not come to pass; and it will not. But a far greater catastrophe and a far darker dark ages were at hand. Yet in face of the prospect of the international war which even now threatens to turn the English into a people of the ruins, Chesterton had nothing to offer; and all that the common man asked of politics was a way of escape from this doom.

4

CHESTERTON accepted the Marxist analysis of the contradiction of the capitalist economic system; in *The Outline of Sanity* he laid it bare with a clarity often unknown to professional economists:

"Capitalism is contradictory as soon as it is complete; because it is dealing with the mass of men in two opposite ways at once. When most men are wage-earners, it is more and more difficult for most men to be customers. For the capitalist is always trying to cut down what his servant demands, and in doing so is cutting down what his customer can spend. As soon as his business is in any difficulties, as at present in the coal business, he tries to reduce what he has to spend on wages, and in doing so reduces what others have to spend on coal. He is wanting the same man to be rich and poor at the same time. This contradiction in capitalism does not appear in the earlier stages, because there are still populations not reduced to the common proletarian condition. But as soon as the wealthy as a whole are employing the wage-earners as a whole, this contradiction stares them in the face like an ironic doom and judgement."

We must be forgiven for starting a chapter with such a long extract, since it conveys so clearly what far longer books have failed to convey at all. Chesterton accepted the Marxist analysis of the contradiction of capitalist society, up to the point at which trusts emerge as the characteristic features of the industrial landscape; and from this he deduced the approaching collapse of the system. Unfortunately, when that collapse did not take place, he forbore to pursue the argument further. When, in Germany, things reached such a pass that the German people in despair put themselves and their economics alike into the hands of a dictator; when that dictator solved the problem of stagnation and unemployment by the simple method of massive rearmament—when, in other words, he set the wheels of industry turning again by the production of goods that no one need buy—all Chesterton could see was the resurrection of "Prussian" devildom. No country had shown itself capable of finding a creative way out of the impasse; when the waving of the Swastika gave it the excuse it was with an audible sigh of relief that the rest of Europe set about overcoming the same problem in precisely the same way: but all this was nothing to Chesterton. Seeing nothing in Hitlerism but the reappearance of the hereditary Prussian disease, he could see nothing in Baldwinism but the sharpening of the surgeon's scalpel. He would, had he lived, have welcomed the operation at present being repeated.

Thereby he dammed up the hopes of Distributism. Since the bankruptcy he predicted did not come to pass in the way he predicted, his message lost all its urgency in the ears of the common man; he abandoned the influence he might have exerted over those who grew up in the despondency of the 1920's to—of all people—the communists. For Communism did promise, at one time, a way out of war: and it was for this reason that the post-war generation turned to it. Its historians declared, and appeared to demonstrate, that there were forces at work in the world making irreversibly for good, that is, for peace: and so great was the intoxication of surrender to these forces that few realized at once whither they were being borne; few realized that the triumphal arch which seemed so near lay beyond the very chasm it was thought to span, and that the communist was indeed, as he proudly proclaimed, not a Christian—because he was not "concerned with the body as well as the soul".

But Chesterton was compelled to dam the hopes of Distributism in another way than this. It is impossible to advocate the manufacture of armaments *and* the abolition of industrialism, the centralized control by the state demanded of modern war *and* the decentralization of community; it is impossible to support at one and the same time rearmament and Distributism. If rearmament is an immediate necessity, then the distributist programme must be deferred indefinitely. If Distributism is an immediate necessity, then some means of national defence other than war must be devised. One contemporary writer, who preaches, under the name of "anarchism", an ideal rather similar to Chesterton's, goes so far as to say that "the abolition of the state and the creation of a co-operative commonwealth" naturally imply Pacifism: "if pacifism is not possible, then anarchism is not possible" (Herbert Read: "The Necessity of Anarchism", in *The Adelphi*, Sept.–Nov., 1937). This conclusion Chesterton rejected; he preferred rearmament to Distributism.

To represent his choice in such terms, however, is of course to misrepresent it. What he really preferred was the England that actually exists, with all its imperfections and possibilities of improvement, to an England subordinated to the imperialism of Germany; and he believed that only by a temporary intensification of armaments, if need be by war, could this England be saved.

§

Chesterton was a patriot in the highest and truest sense. No understanding of him is possible unless this is understood. But true patriotism is a very rare thing—so rare that it is generally mistaken for unpatriotism. True patriotism has nothing to do with racialism, or imperialism or the idolatry of the nation-state. The ideal of all these things is a uniformity, and is derived from the abstracting intellect; but patriotism springs from the imagination and delights in particularity. "If patriotism does not mean a defined and declared preference for certain traditions or surroundings, it means nothing whatever" ("The Patriotic Idea" in *England a Nation*, edited by L. Oldershaw). It is not a devotion to something afar, but to something very near: the very essence of patriotism is that the traditions and surroundings should be those which a man knows best—those in which he was brought up. Therefore it cannot be an uncritical devotion. True patriotism is intensely critical; it judges the traditions of its country continually, and is as unsparing in its denunciations of the bad as it is passionate in its loyalty to the good. If patriotism demanded a wholesale approval, if it demanded a blinding of eyes to the truth, if it demanded of men that they should perform acts abhorrent to their consciences, then no good Christian could be a patriot.

Chesterton was both a good patriot and a good Christian. It was for this reason that he detested imperialism—and not only German imperialism. When he denounced the German invasion of Belgium in 1914, he was in a far stronger position than most of those in this country who did so, because he had already denounced the British invasion of the Transvaal. "The annexation of the Transvaal", he had written ten years before, "was a crime committed against the European virtue of patriotism. For a man has clearly no more right to say that his British patriotism obliges him to destroy the Boer nation than he has to say that his sense of the sanctity of marriage makes him run away with his neighbour's wife" (*op. cit.*). Naturally, he had been stigmatized as "unpatriotic".

"A thing like the British Empire," he had written, "which contains Dutchmen and Negroes and Chinamen in Hong Kong, may be a perfectly legitimate object of a certain kind of intellectual esteem, but it is ludicrous to call it patriotism, or invoke the ancient deities of the hearth and the river and the hill" (*op. cit.*). As it was this intellectual esteem that distinguished imperialism from Chesterton's patriotism, so it was this that distinguishes what has come to be called nationalism from what he meant by the word. When he spoke of nationalism, and called it the spiritual demand of a healthy man, he meant "a particular relation to some homogeneous community of manageable and imaginable size, large enough to inspire his reverence by its hold on history and small enough to inspire his affection by its hold on himself" (*op. cit.*). The nation was, for him, essentially a community small enough to be experienced—the smaller the better. It was a unity that appealed not so much to the intellect as to the heart and the imagination. As such, it might well be a unity in multiplicity, like a work of art. Nor would it, I think, be unfair to Chesterton to define the England he loved as a multiplicity of local traditions bound together in one common tradition—of freedom. As he was the lifelong champion of the rights of small nations themselves, so he was the champion of local patriotisms within the nations: for he perceived in both a return to personal and immediate relationships with people and things, from that impersonal and mechanized relationship which is the curse of the modern world:

> "We have reached in the modern world a condition of such appalling unreality that everything is done on

paper. Men know the destiny of countries when they have never met a native, and profess love and hatred for men whom, if they saw them in the street, they could not tell from Poles or Portuguese" (*op. cit.*).

It is another example of that all-pervading "abstractionism" to which we have referred already. And the cure?—

"We must at all costs get back to smaller political entities, because we must at all costs get back to reality. We must get nearer and nearer again to love and hate and mother-wit, to personal judgements and the truth in the faces of men" (*op. cit.*).

§

It was in loyalty to such a view of nationalism that Chesterton supported the war of 1914–18, and would have supported a greater. No stronger case against Pacifism has ever been voiced than that which is to be found in his *Autobiography*, because it is based upon facts and sentiments which the average pacifist ignores almost as completely as the average nationalist. The war, he said, was not fought to end war; it was not fought to make the world safe for political democracy; it was fought to defend the local customs and immemorial traditions of England: and it succeeded in its object.

The natural retort to this argument, that the war was, in fact, fought to defend and extend vested interests in the colonies, is obviously inadequate. That the war of 1914–18 was the natural outcome of the economic situation of the world at that time is true: but if it can be shown that it defended other things besides vested interests—valuable things—the things, in fact, for which the actual soldiers actually killed and were killed, then that truth is irrelevant. If it can be shown that the victory of 1918 was a dual victory, for Allied patriotism as much as for Allied finance, still it is irrelevant: the victory would have seemed worth while to those who won it. The economic argument only becomes all-important if it can be shown that Allied patriotism won less than Allied capitalism. If that is the truth, then the war was, indeed, from the standpoint of those who won it, a ghastly failure: for capitalism, as Chesterton demonstrated and patriotism knows, is the mortal enemy of all local customs and immemorial traditions whatever; it is the enemy of all creative life.

The demonstration of such a truth, however, can never be conclusive; and from the experience of the past twenty years different conclusions may, perhaps, be drawn. One conclusion only is unavoidable, and that is that in her relations with the defeated countries England betrayed the ideals of those who had fought in the name of patriotism more grossly than a nation had ever betrayed the ideals of its youth before: because never before had a nation's youth been so decimated that few or none were left to arraign it. France and England after the war set out, deliberately, to reduce the German people to penury, to ignominy and at last to despair. "The men whose names are written on the Beaconsfield War Memorial died to prevent Beaconsfield being so immediately overshadowed by Berlin that all its reforms would be modelled on Berlin, all its products used for the international purposes of Berlin, even if the King of Prussia were not called in so many words the Suzerain of the King of England. They died to prevent it and they did prevent it" (*Autobiography*). True, but they did not, because they could not prevent Berlin from being so overshadowed by London and Paris; they did not, because they could not prevent Germany from being reduced to a vassal state, "retaining merely a formal independence, and in every vital matter steered by the diplomacy and penetrated by the culture of the conqueror" (*op. cit.*). If England committed a crime against the European virtue of patriotism when she annexed the Transvaal, how great was the crime committed when she so treated every just demand of the German people, when they were beaten and unarmed, that they finally became convinced that all morality between nations was a fraud, and that nothing of their own would ever be had that was not had by force?

But patriotism is not an occasional virtue; and it is inherently impossible that a nation should act so unpatriotically in its foreign relations as England did after the war, and yet remain patriotic in its domestic concerns. For, whatever jingoes and cosmopolitans may say to the contrary, Chesterton was right when he declared that true patriotism and true internationalism are complementary. As a fact, in the Hall of Mirrors at Versailles England saw herself as she really was. The imperialism which, when the evil traditions of Germany were destroyed, trampled the innocent underfoot, had its counterpart in a commercialism at home that left, where it left them at all, the local customs and immemorial traditions of our country as survivals merely. There is only one way of saving these, and that is by means of a social revolution; but there was not the moral energy left in England after the war to carry such a revolution through; and by the time that a new generation had arisen, the fatal actions of the old were bearing their fruits—in the nemesis we are confronted with to-day.

§

To Chesterton, labouring almost alone to awaken his country to the need of undoing, and not over-doing, the evil of capitalism, the truth should surely have been plain, that modern war, the war in which a whole nation's energies are unremittingly engaged, so decimates those who wage it at the front and corrupts those who support it at the back that nothing, save by a miracle, can result from it but an endless moral deterioration. And yet he was blind to this corruption. What he would not admit on the economic level, he could not perceive on the spiritual: namely, that war is the extension and intensification of capitalism. It is in time of war that the depersonalization of society, which is the spiritual concomitant of capitalism, reaches its maximum; it is in time of war that creative activity is everywhere at a nadir; above all, it is in time of war that men are stirred up as at no other to regard whole nations of men, women and children whom they have never seen as superhuman, worthy only of love, or sub-human, worthy only of hate.

Could he have seen it, however, he would have seen his own campaign in its true perspective, and thereby restored to it all the urgency which it had lost in the ears of the common man. "The only way out of danger", he had written in *The Outline of Sanity*, "is the dangerous way. The sort of call that must be made on the modern English is the sort of call that is made before a great war or a great revolution." That is truer to-day than when it was written; and never before has the course he advocated, for withstanding "the lifelessness which the machine imposes on the masses", been more imperatively demanded. For, whether the international war we are waging results in barbarism or totalitarianism, whether it turns the English into a people of the ruins or England into a servile state, there is no way to cure or prevent it save by such a return to reality and personal judgements as Chesterton held to be the one necessity. Voluntary communities of men and women, dedicated to re-establishing a right relationship with the earth and with one another, may prove nuclei for a new colonization of a wilderness, or they may provide the dynamic for a repersonalization of the social machine, but in either case they are the best hope of resisting the steady moral degeneration. In such communities at least an effort can be made, however desperate or forlorn, to declare the validity of the individual in the very ecstasy of self-immolation, and in the very teeth of destruction to create.

But such a course of action in time of war implies a refusal to take part in war; it implies Pacifism—and that, as we have seen, Chesterton rejected. For reasons which should now be obvious, that rejection seems to us to have been his greatest mistake. Pacifism was, we believe, the logical outcome of both his politics and his patriotism; and it was more than that: it was the natural consummation of his ethics. In Pacifism not only his reason but his imagination might have been satisfied, his activity have been totally suffused by his religion. His refusal of it places him in sudden contrast to the only other churchman of his day with whom it is at all natural to compare him: the late Canon Sheppard. There is more than a superficial likeness between them in other respects. Both owed their popularity and influence largely to their humour; and their humour was of fundamentally the same kind—the kind that Carlyle called "the purest effluence of a deep, fine and loving nature". Both built up quasi-political movements on an unsectarian religious basis, and in doing so, each was consciously emphasizing an element of Christ's teaching. The elements are complementary, as the parts of an organic whole must always be; and in practice each is the justification of the other. A complete Pacifism in capitalist society can be nothing less than revolutionary: a revolutionary movement that does not abjure violence becomes an accomplice in the thing it abhors.[1]

Nevertheless, Chesterton refused the pacifist solution, as Sheppard appears to have refused the distributist. "Refusal", however, is really too positive a name for his reaction. The truth is that he never faced up to the pacifist position at all. Throughout the collection of essays entitled *The End of the Armistice*, he treats under the name of "pacifism" that mere reluctance to make war, that sentiment for peace, which was in this country the backwash of 1918. Chesterton knew the meaning of love; and knowing it could only have been repelled by this simulacrum of it that used to prevail so widely in circles calling themselves pacifist: the self-mortification that passed for self-sacrifice: the turning of the other cheek which was farther from forgiveness than is anger: for anger has this at least in common with genuine compassion, that it is spontaneous. As Keats said, "a quarrel in the streets is a thing to be hated, but the energies displayed in it are fine". No doubt Chesterton would have relished a street-fight. Indeed, he described one with gusto in his autobiography. No doubt he respected the anger and defiance that find expression in battle, just as he respected the desire for security that exists in every man. Yet one of his valuable achievements was his disclosure of the injustice to which this last, in itself innocent, desire was leading, in a competitive, mechanized society; and he showed that a new consciousness was necessary to man if he was not to be made the slave of the

[1] See Note II at the end of this book.

machine: a giant's awareness to manipulate the limbs of a giant.

A new consciousness will indeed be required. But it is the machine linked to anger and defiance, and not directly to the desire for security, that is destroying the remains of Christian civilization. It will be the executor of an injustice, and one intolerable to the democratic imagination, but one far greater than Chesterton dreamed. For there is no crime of oppression, destitution or unemployment that can outweigh that wholesale massacre or starvation of the innocents, which is the quintessence of modern war. It was his sense of this violation of the democratic emotion that made Canon Sheppard a pacifist; and his Pacifism, and that of the best of his followers, differs by a whole world of religious experience from the false "pacifism" we have been discussing. It differs from it in being prepared for the most radical sacrifices known to man: in being prepared, if need be, to lay down its life not only for its friend but for its enemy.

§

"We have used fire and sword, death and destruction, slander and surrender, diplomacy and flattery, suspicion and oblivion, to solve the supposed problem of Germany; and we find that we still have not solved the problem of Prussia. The reason is that the thing involved belongs to the history of thought, to the thousand sects and philosophies, rather than to the relatively recent imperial divisions of history. The thing is not a nation; it is rather a religion or perhaps an irreligion."

Thus wrote Chesterton in *The End of the Armistice:* and is not the corollary obvious? If all these methods have failed, would it not be wiser, not to say more Christian, to try the method of generous treatment? That was Canon Sheppard's conclusion.

It may or may not be true that Prussia stands for the evil element in Germany, inasmuch as it has long embodied the particular antichristian temptations that haunt that country. Probably it is true, since, for good geographical and historical reasons, Prussia was always less exposed than any other part of Germany to the civilizing influence of Rome. But the question, which Chesterton never attempted to answer, is why this element should at times—and especially at the present time—be allowed by the rest of Germany to "become its spearhead, or to use it like a spear"; on his own admission, the tribal element "only occasionally drives the Germans". This question Chesterton never answered, because to have done so would have meant admitting, not merely the inefficacy of the methods he had listed for exorcizing prussianism, but their absolute antagonism to the true ones. The nearest he came to admitting it was when he declared that prussianism was an idea or irreligion, that could only be countered by a truer idea or a real religion: in other words, by a "change of heart"—to use the expression beloved of those English journalists who pressed for an even harsher treaty and more prolonged starvation of Germany after the last war. But when he showed that Christendom was faced in these latter days by the same challenge of paganism that it had overcome in its earliest, he would not allow that the methods used to overcome it by the early Christians might still be the best.

"Truth can understand error, but error cannot understand truth." That phrase has for its natural counterpart another: "tout comprendre, c'est tout pardonner"; and these two between them sum up, for me, all that is most vital in Chesterton's genius. He could laugh at his opponents, because he loved them; he loved them because he forgave them; and he forgave them because he understood them: he had room for them in his superior vision even when they had none for him in their inferior. But if this is the truth, he betrayed his genius by his attitude towards Germany. It is no accident that there is little humour in *The Barbarism of Berlin* or *The End of the Armistice*. He made no attempt to understand Germany; he treated it always as a *deus*, or rather a *diabolus ex machina*, projecting on to an abstraction called "the Prussian" all the tendencies he despised. No wonder he was unable to perceive the corruption spread by war! —And yet, to see how that Germany came into being, to see the causes, spiritual and economic, that precipitated it, is to be so tempted to repentance and forgiveness that the reaction which, we have said, Chesterton's politics alone would have dictated, becomes the natural emotion of our hearts.

Pacifism is the politics of forgiveness—of forgiveness raised, as Mr. Middleton Murry has said, "from a private virtue to the virtue of nations" (in *The Brotherhood of Peace*, Peace Pledge Union, 1939). Had Chesterton given his allegiance to the great English pacifist movement, his life-work would, I believe, have been fulfilled. It was his triumph that he remained, nearly always, the spokesman of the highest aspirations of his country: it is in virtue of this fact that he can be called, at one and the same time, a conservative like Browning and a revolutionary like Blake—he was, in fact, his own supreme paradox. It was his tragedy that he did not aspire beyond those aspirations, to become the prophet of a perhaps unrealizable attainment: if, indeed, forgiveness does lie beyond the realization of England. There is no one who can be sure even of that; and certain it is that no great moral advance has ever been made by the mass of mankind that was not expected of it almost as a natural consummation by the few. Had Chesterton given his allegiance to Pacifism, his genius would finally have prevailed over his "character", the Christianity he served over the common sense for which he was admired: for it is Christianity, and not common sense, that "preaches an impossibility and tries to make it come true".

POSTSCRIPT

WRITING about G. K. Chesterton is like climbing a mountain. The end seems continually to be in sight, or to lie just over the next crest; always when the crest is reached another unfolds itself beyond that. And at last one is forced to leave off out of sheer fatigue, and because the daylight is all but spent. Yet with every fresh ridge surmounted a new and wider prospect is opened up, until all that has been accomplished seems, in the fresh perspective, narrow and insignificant. Chesterton is like church doctrine itself: he can be participated in on many different levels of understanding. At the lowest, his truths shatter into contradictions, acceptable only as perversities. At the highest, they are discovered to be, if not completely comprehensive, within their limits perfect, portions of an organic whole.

Tolstoy once said that there were three things necessary to an artist: "that he should stand on a level with the highest life-conception of his time, that he should experience feeling and have the desire and capacity to transmit it, and that he should moreover have a talent for one of the forms of art."

In the first section of this essay I suggested that Chesterton, by giving his allegiance to the Roman Catholic Church, fell below the level of the highest life-conception of his time and country. For that only is the highest which comprehends all knowledge and all experience, however contradictory. Religion, like wit, "sees the consistency in things"; it is the discovery of a unity in diversity; the final reconciliation of contraries. Chesterton did in some measure what he accused the Buddhists of doing—and in the measure to which he accused them of doing it—he restricted the diversity to preserve a unity.

In my second section I contrasted Chesterton's desire with his capacity to transmit feeling: asserting, nevertheless, that he did often succeed in his purpose, which was the purpose of all art—for art is a paradigm of religion—that of revealing the unity in multiplicity. Each of his works is an organic unity: the whole is implicit in each one of its parts.

But what applies to his individual productions applies to his achievement as a whole. To present his viewpoint becomes, therefore, inordinately difficult; "a kind of huge helplessness" overtakes one. Since to separate any one strand of his thought and treat it in isolation is immediately to impoverish it. Yet to link up each with all the others, save by implication, would be a superhuman task, involving endless repetition and final formlessness. In my third section I called criticism the art for which Chesterton had the greatest talent, and implied thereby that a work of criticism is a work of art. It cannot therefore be formless. What the imagination discovers imagination must reveal; and imagination cannot work freely on the particulars until it sees them in the perspective of the whole.

Not only literary, but social criticism was the chosen field of Chesterton's genius. In my third and fourth sections I have studied the application of his principles, first to the domestic and then to the foreign concerns of his country. The topic has proved more topical than I anticipated when I began. On all sides now (1939) people are quoting an observation of Chesterton's posthumously republished:

> "The Prussian patriot may plaster himself all over with eagles and iron crosses, but he will be found in

practice side by side with the Red Flag. The Prussian and the Russian will agree about everything; especially about Poland" (*The End of the Armistice*).

Not everybody who has quoted these words, however, has remembered those which immediately follow them: "They may differ in many things, but in hatred of the Christian civilization they are truly international"; yet without these, his prophecy is insignificant. We have to know all that Chesterton implied by the term, "Christian civilization". My object has been to throw some light on this. If, in doing so, I have seemed to take Chesterton more seriously than he took himself—at least I am unlikely to be accused of trying to break a butterfly upon a wheel!

As my understanding of him has grown, and my imagination been enriched by it, so has my admiration. Now that this essay is finished, I see him towering before me, a figure of portentous stature; and I know not only that what I have written is woefully inadequate—that was inevitable—but that all I have tried to write is inadequate, too. The most fundamental, the unique quality of his genius has eluded my clumsiness to the last. The light which he turned upon the world he turned upon himself also: not merely its objectivity and charity, but its humour. His "character" at its best was, in fact, of the same order as his art and wit. It was the delight of a great man in his own personality.

NOTES

NOTE I (Page 23).

The "complete anthropology repudiating the supernatural," which I had in mind when writing this essay, was that sketched by John Middleton Murry in his book *God: an introduction to the Science of Metabiology* (Cape, 1929). Although my criticism of Chesterton's standpoint still seems to me substantially correct, I would not now express the unqualified allegiance to Mr. Murry's Metabiology that I did seven years ago.

In the recently published Letters of Max Plowman (*Bridge into the Future*, Dakars, 1944), I find the following statement: " Blake was a supernaturalist in the sense that he could see Nature as the expression of something greater than itself; but Murry wants Nature to be self-sufficient, which to my mind is just like wanting a work of art to disown the hand that made it. It *is* itself and in a sense self-sufficient. It is also the expression of something greater than itself " (Letter of Nov. 20, 1933). This seems to me a true criticism of Murry's former Pantheism—unsatisfactory word !—and it implies a faith more nearly akin to Orthodox Christianity than Max Plowman himself may have realised: how nearly I have tried to define in a forthcoming book, *The Tree of Knowledge*.

This essay on Chesterton was completed during the early months of the War, and bears traces of its date both in its references to public events and the absence of reference to several valuable works on Chesterton published since—Maisie Ward's monumental biography in particular. I hope the reader will take this as a partial excuse for the many defects which only a drastic rehandling could set right.

NOTE II (Page 85).

The synthesis between the intuitions of G. K. Chesterton and Canon Sheppard, suggested in this section, was perfectly achieved by Eric Gill, whose writings were virtually unknown to me when this book was written. Gill was both a distributist and a pacifist professed: and a great Christian into the bargain. A remark of his recounted to me by the late Max Plowman may perhaps appropriately be put on record here. Gill was at work on his autobiography at the time. "I cannot imagine", he remarked to Max, "a more fitting end to the life of a great man than Gilbert Chesterton's, whose autobiography was only just completed when he passed away." It was less than three months later that, having just put the final touches to his own lovely record of a creative life, Eric Gill went to join the friend whom he had described in it as "a writer and as a holy man, beyond all his contemporaries".

www.ingramcontent.com/pod-product-compliance
Lightning Source LLC
Chambersburg PA
CBHW070323100426
42743CB00011B/2529